at the
WATER'S
EDGE

at the WATER'S EDGE

gardening with moisture-loving plants

PHILIP SWINDELLS

WARD LOCK LTD · LONDON

First published in Great Britain in 1988
by Ward Lock Limited, 8 Clifford Street
London W1X 1RB, an Egmont Company

House editor Denis Ingram
Designed by Anita Ruddell

Text filmset/set in ITC Garamond Light 11/12pt
by Columns of Reading
Printed and bound in Portugal by Resopal

British Library Cataloguing in Publication Data

Swindells, Philip
    At the water's edge : gardening with
    moisture-loving plants.
    1. Gardening
    I. Title
    635

ISBN 0–7063–6645–X

Frontispiece: *A shady spot beside a woodland stream is enlivened by colourful primulas and the bold foliage of rodgersias.*

CONTENTS

Preface *page 6*

■ **1** ■
The Bog Garden *page 8*

■ **2** ■
Bog Plants *page 20*

■ **3** ■
Stream and Poolside *page 40*

■ **4** ■
Plants for Stream and Poolside *page 48*

■ **5** ■
The Peat Garden *page 68*

■ **6** ■
Peat-loving Plants *page 78*

■ **7** ■
Ferns and Mosses *page 96*

APPENDIX ONE
Plant Problems *page 112*

APPENDIX TWO
Increasing Your Plants *page 116*

APPENDIX THREE
Moisture-loving Plants *page 120*

Index *page 126*

Acknowledgements *page 128*

PREFACE

There have been many books written about the water garden, but none has addressed the planting of the immediate surroundings, nor considered fully the opportunities offered by a stream or rill. There are so many fine plants that can be grown in such situations, and many different ways of coping with the often unusual conditions. A review of this aspect of gardening is long overdue.

Associated with this we quite naturally have ferns, those cool, green, unsung heroes of moist places; and they lead us quite naturally into the peat garden. A different damp environment, but one that is also often found at the water's edge.

To me the plants of damp places are a joy. Bogs, swamps, marshes and streamsides are a perpetual pleasure; places where nature is at its most luxuriant and diverse. I hope that this book will enable you to share some of these delights with me.

P.S.

Iris, marsh marigolds and the golden-flowered ranunculus watch over a tranquil pool of waterlilies.

CHAPTER ONE

THE BOG GARDEN

A bog garden gives the imaginative gardener tremendous opportunities to grow plants that are difficult to manage successfully under more regular garden conditions. A number of plants that many of us struggle with in the herbaceous border prosper when provided with a constant supply of moisture – astilbes, hostas and loosestrife for example.

□ The natural bog □

When provided with the opportunity to plant a naturally wet area as a bog garden, most gardeners are initially enthused. However, once they start work on such a project they often become rapidly disillusioned, for a natural bog is difficult to plant and manage successfully without a lot of careful thought and effort.

Before lifting a spade in preparation, it is vital to establish that the wet area is really wet, and wet all the year around. Discover how it is that it has become so wet in the first place. Is it a naturally low lying area, in which case in dry summers it may not remain wet; or is it a part of the garden which deliberately receives land drainage water, in which case it could be excessively wet at some periods and much drier at others. Is it spring fed? If so, are you likely to divert or disrupt the spring by cultivations? All these questions need to be addressed before work commences. Indeed, all are critical factors to consider at the pre-planning stage.

The gardener who has a well cultivated, naturally wet area, is fortunate indeed, for with constancy of water supply he can go ahead and plant his bog. The untamed wet area is a very different proposition. Here troublesome weeds, including rushes and sedges, are likely to abound, weeds that will have been seeding themselves in the same place for many years. Most semi-aquatic plants, especially rushes and reeds, have the capability of remaining viable as seed in soggy ground for a number of years, so as soon as you disturb the soil they will germinate freely.

□ Weed control □

Weed cover on wet land is not easy to remove physically. Most is deeply rooted or tussock forming and clings to the wet soil. Try taking out large, wet, soggy clumps of weed and you will find a generous quantity of top soil goes with it.

Chemical herbicides can be used, but you need to think well ahead as they are relatively slow acting in ensuring total destruction of the plant tissue.

Plants that live in wet areas, especially the weed flora, also tend to have glossy waterproof foliage which does not accept sprayed herbicides very well. A sticking agent is essential, such as washing up liquid or, in the case of weeds like mare's tail, an additive to break down the protective waxy coating of the foliage. For mare's tail, the addition of 25% by volume of ordinary household paraffin to a regularly mixed spray of a systemic herbicide containing glyphosate, ensures that sufficient absorption takes place.

While herbicides will kill pernicious semi-aquatic weeds, they have to remain in contact with the plant tissue for several hours to be wholly effective.

Apart from the limitations of their use on difficult foliage, careful consideration must be given to the application of herbicides on wet land, especially if the dampness of the soil is associated with a water course or other aquatic feature. Residual herbicides can cause immense environmental damage in wet areas and should be excluded, especially when planting has to be undertaken soon after clearance. Systemic herbicides are generally more satisfactory as they are mostly inactivated on contact with the soil, but care should be taken to ensure that they do not linger as a residue in a weak solution of standing water.

■ *Systemic herbicides*

If a systemic herbicide is to be used, and for the most part this is the most sensible route to take, then the timing of the application will be vital. Such herbicides work on the principle of being absorbed by the plant tissue and then translocated around the sap stream, killing the plant completely without polluting the soil. The herbicide need only come into contact with a portion of the foliage in order to be totally effective. This is in contrast to the more traditional contact killers which depend upon blanket coverage of the foliage for a complete kill.

As a systemic herbicide depends upon effective translocation around the sap stream of the plant, the most effective and speedy kill will result from a spring application when the weeds are burgeoning into growth. At this time the plentiful leafy cover is also most receptive to herbicide application.

Although this means of weed killing provides a total kill which does not pollute the site, it does demand a degree of patience, for systemic herbicides take several weeks to work effectively.

Do not be disheartened if nothing much appears to happen for the first couple of weeks. Resist the temptation of seeking rapid action by applying a contact killer. Burning off the foliage will reduce the effectiveness of a previously applied systemic herbicide and may result in an incomplete kill, particularly of hidden underground root systems. It should also be remembered that although the herbicide will kill plants completely, their destroyed tissue will remain brown and intact for some time. This is often difficult to cope with, for many of the pernicious weeds of damp places are tough and tussock forming. While it may be desirable to remove all the brown foliage debris early on, it is more prudent to leave it for a few weeks to allow it to start decomposing. When you observe foliage rotting, and the tussocks of clump-forming plants have become loose and detach readily, then the entire area can be scarified with a strong rake, and the old vegetation removed. Cultivation can then commence.

Fig. 1 *Trenching.*

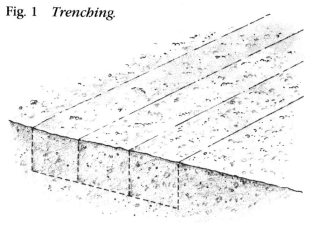

(a) Sequence of rows to be dug.

(b) The first row is inverted upon itself.

(c) The second row is inverted upon the first.

(d) The third row is inverted in the trench created by the removal of the second row. This is repeated until the plot is dug.

□ Preparing the land □

Traditionally digging is undertaken during the winter, the purpose being to turn the soil over when the majority of plants have finished their life cycle. Also, frost can weather the soil and break it down into a crumbly tilth for the spring. With a naturally wet area, however, this is impossible, especially on heavy clay soil. During the winter when the soil is saturated, none but the toughest gardener is able to turn over such weighty spadefuls.

■ *Trenching*

For land that has not been cultivated for a number of years, trenching is the best technique to use. This involves turning over the first row of soil as if single digging (Fig. 1). Invert the next row on the top, thereby revealing a trench. Then turn each successive row into the trench, being sure to invert it completely in order to smother any seedling weeds. When you arrive at the end of the plot, you will still have an open trench. Despite the fact that most books tell you otherwise, there is no need to panic.

This poolside is given an oriental feel by the clever use of statuary and native plants of the Far East.

Fig. 2 *Construction of composite pool and bog garden.*

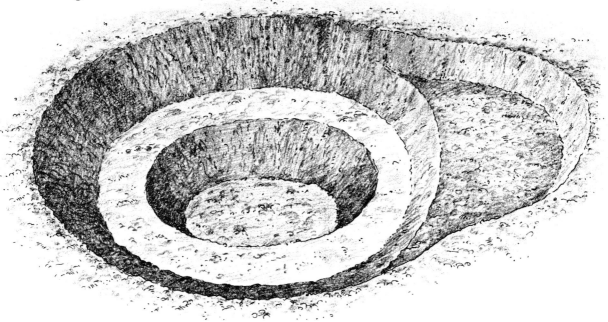

(a) Excavate the pool with an additional shallow area to provide a bog garden. For the best effect the bog area should be about one-third of the surface area of the adjacent pool.

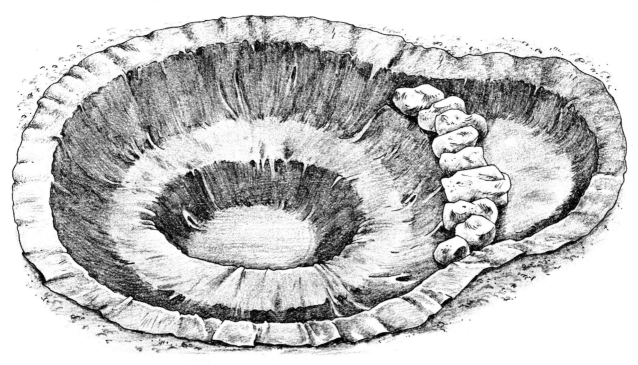

(b) Install the liner carefully, following the contours of the bog feature. The pool should be divided from the bog garden by a line of stones. These should not emerge higher than the surrounding ground.

In theory the first row of digging should have been removed entirely and transferred to the other end of the area to be dug, thus revealing a trench. The digging sequence described above would then follow. However, removing soil from one end of the plot to the other is rather tedious, so as the finished area is ultimately going to be raked and levelled, there seems no harm in having one row at the end of the plot slightly higher than the remainder for the period during which the soil is going to be allowed to weather.

Ideally newly broken land should be upturned from the early summer, following herbicide treatment, until the next spring. This allows the soil to weather properly, any old decaying roots or vestiges of tussock-forming plants to be removed, and ample opportunity to destroy seedlings resulting from the germination of long dormant seeds. In most cases this time scale will not be acceptable. When this is the case, be prepared for a good deal more maintenance work, especially in the early stages.

Apart from preparation of the existing soil, it is beneficial to incorporate some additional organic matter. Most low-lying areas accumulate a disproportionate amount of organic material and clearly the majority of moisture-loving plants benefit from it. So for preference use coarse moss peat, but where this proves to be too expensive, then use well rotted leaves or animal manure, but not from animals bedded on sawdust or shavings.

□ Constructing a bog □

Gardeners who do not have a naturally wet area, usually construct their bog garden as an extension of a water garden feature. Not only do bog plants quite naturally associate with such a feature, they also provide a link with the surrounding garden and enable the harsh edge of the pool to be disguised more subtly.

Constructing a bog garden in conjunction with a pool (Fig. 2) is not too difficult if its development is envisaged when the pool and its immediate

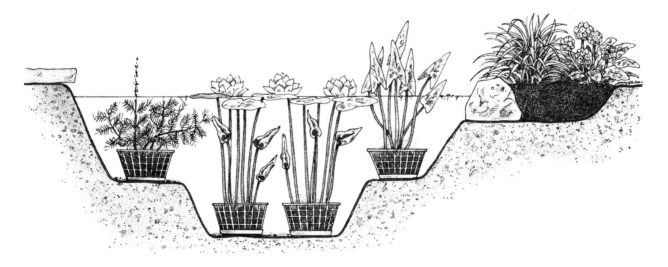

(c) The bog garden area should be filled with a suitable compost, using the stones to prevent it from slipping into the pool. Top dressing the area with pea shingle is an optional extra.

Above: *Astilbes froth and foam at the streamside, the bold leaves of gunnera providing a focal point in the background.*
Opposite: *Contrasts of foliage beside the water and at its edge. The circular leaves of* Peltiphyllum *smile upon the spiky foliage of the golden club.*

Fig. 3 *Construction of bog garden.*

(a) Excavate the bog area to an even depth of 30–45 cm (12–18 in), and remove any sharp stones which could puncture the lining.

(b) Line the pool with a flexible liner, securing the top so that later it can be disguised.

(c) Fill with suitable moisture-retentive soil mixture, covering the overlap; water well and then plant. This stage shows the bog garden fully planted up.

surroundings are planned, preferably before construction commences. Adding a bog garden afterwards is fraught with difficulties, although this is the only method of creating such a feature when the pool is made of fibre glass or pre-formed plastic. When a liner is used, then it is merely a question of purchasing a liner larger than required for the pool and incorporating the bog garden at the edge as if it were a spreading shallow pool.

■ Pool liners

A pool liner is a sheet of heavy gauge rubber, PVC or polythene material which is placed in an excavation and moulded to its contours to form a waterproof lining. In the case of a pool, great care is needed to install the liner so that it does not wrinkle or puncture. While the appearance of the liner is not critical in a bog garden, as it should be completely hidden, some of the precautions taken when installing it, whether as an extension of a water feature, or as a separate bog garden feature (Fig. 3), are as necessary as when building a pool.

The selection of a suitable liner is equally important for there are a number of different qualities, each with different virtues. Those in the lower price range are usually of 500 gauge polythene in a sky-blue colour and made in a number of standard sizes. These are mass produced, very cheap, and available from most major supermarkets as well as nurseries and garden centres. While they have considerable limitations when used for pool construction these are not so readily apparent in the independent bog garden, although it has to be said that such liners are almost impossible to use in a dual pool and bog garden situation.

When used for a pool, any exposed area of liner quickly succumbs to sunlight damage, the area between water surface and ground level becoming bleached, cracking and quickly disintegrating. This obviously happens more easily when a liner is used to extend a pool into a bog garden, for however cleverly contrived this extension turns out to be, almost inevitably some of the polythene will be visible. When the bog garden is a separate entity, then the polythene can be concealed completely and no problems will occur. Neither do they with PVC liners or those made of Butyl rubber.

Both of these materials are excellent for pool and bog garden construction, or a combination of the two. The rubber kind is the most durable, but also the most expensive and where an independent bog garden is to be constructed, then it may be more prudent to settle for the less expensive, but perfectly functional PVC liner.

■ Calculating size

Having decided upon the type of liner to be employed, it is then necessary to calculate the size. Do not skimp on the size of the bog garden. If it is going to be an extension of the pool feature, then to present a balance it needs to cover a similar area. In addition to the amount needed for the pool, you will require a length comprising the total 'floor' area of the bog garden, the accumulation of totals for depth (the minimum being 30 cm or 12 in at any one point) and an allowance for overlap.

■ Excavation

The excavation of a bog garden, when forming part of a water garden feature, must be undertaken at the same time as the pool and should form a spreading shallow 'pool' no less than 30 cm (12 in) deep, although it is not necessary to

go any deeper than 45 cm (18 in). Similar care should be exercised when constructing a bog garden as when lining a pool, for the introduction of the liner is to ensure that the garden remains water tight. It is therefore sensible to scour the bog garden extension, along with the pool, for sharp sticks or stones that are likely to puncture the liner. On gravelly soils, or those where flints are troublesome, it is advisable to scatter a generous layer of sand over the base of the bog garden area and provide well dampened wads of newspaper for the sides. This will hopefully ensure that the liner remains intact when the soil mixture is replaced.

■ *Creating boggy conditions*
In the case of a bog garden that is attached to a pool, once the excavation has been lined the areas should be clearly divided by means of a row of bricks or stone. This retaining wall keeps the soil medium out of the pool, but, at the same time, allows water to percolate through to the soil and create boggy conditions, the soil surface being at least 5 cm (2 in) above water level. The mixture that is put in the bog garden area can, in most cases, comprise the excavated soil mixed with a very generous addition of coarse peat or well rotted garden compost or leaf mould.

In other parts of the garden, similar conditions can be provided by excavating an area of border and lining it with a PVC or rubber liner, the excavated soil being prepared as described earlier, and replaced. It must be thoroughly soaked with water from the outset and a close eye kept on it for signs of drying out during periods of hot weather. Indeed, one of the problems created by such a feature being independent of a pool, is the necessity to continually monitor the soil conditions to ensure that they are suitable for the plants being grown.

If a pool is made out of concrete, a bog garden can be attached as a separate basin, or used independently to create a bog garden elsewhere. However, unless you are particularly adept at this form of construction, it is best left to the experts. Certainly it is not a method to be described here.

For most situations, the lined bog garden is best, and an absolute necessity when the feature is to become an integral part of a water garden with a pre-formed plastic or fibreglass pool.

Sentinel-like irises herald the arrival of summer, taking over from the rich reds of late spring-flowering primulas.

CHAPTER TWO

BOG
PLANTS

C hoosing plants for a bog garden can be a difficult task, for nature does not clearly define what a bog plant is. To most of us, however, bog plants are those that like moist conditions, but not standing water, and if treated as ordinary border plants become stunted and foliage scorched unless the growing season is exceptionally wet. Astilbes are fine examples of such plants, struggling under dryish border conditions, but thriving where there is abundant moisture. Unlike true aquatic plants, those of the bog garden are planted in the dormant period, or from containers during the growing season.

□ Harbingers of spring □

When the pool or stream is dull and lifeless during the winter and early spring, the bog garden can maintain our interest. Winter heliotrope, *Petasites fragrans*, starts flowering during the winter and goes on into spring. It produces fragrant lilac-pink blossoms in dense clusters close to the ground, which are succeeded by long stalked, rounded leaves not unlike those of a giant rhubarb. Its larger cousin, *P. japonicus*, is useful for rough or unkempt areas, producing immense, cabbage-like foliage well over 1 m (3 ft) high and half as much across, preceded by large crowded heads of scentless greenish-white blossoms. The hardy umbrella plant, *Peltiphyllum peltatum*, can be grown in similar situations. This is altogether more modest, with globular heads of soft pink flowers on slender stems 45 cm (1 ft 6 in) high. These are followed during summer by rounded bronze-green leaves, supported like an umbrella on a central leaf stalk. Although not strictly spring flowering plants, it is useful to mention the ornamental rhubarbs here, for it is at this time that they are at their most colourful, especially the varieties of *Rheum palmatum*. With broad spreading foliage and flowers that ultimately attain a height of between 1 and 2 m (3 ft 3 in and 6 ft 6 in), it is a giant of a plant. However, its fancy forms like *R.p.* 'Bowles Crimson' and *R.p. tanguticum* have bright purple-red and deeply cut foliage respectively.

■ Globe flowers
The globe flowers or trollius are genuine spring bloomers, with attractive incurved heads of yellow or orange buttercup-like flowers. *Trollius europaeus*, a soft yellow species, and the bold *T. asiaticus* are the parents of most garden hybrids but the cultivars 'Fire Globe', 'Canary Bird' and 'Orange Princess' are

much improved. Where space is limited, the lovely little *T. pumilus*, and, more particularly, the improved 'Wargrave Variety', coupled with the even tinier *T. yunnanensis*, ensure that even the most modest bog garden can accommodate a clump or two of these handsome plants.

■ *Marsh marigolds*

Few people are unfamiliar with the marsh marigold or kingcup, *Caltha palustris*. Although still abundant in the wild in many places, most gardeners do not despise its presence beside the pool or in a damp patch at the streamside, enjoying its attractive hummocks of dark green foliage garlanded in early spring with waxy blooms of intense golden-yellow. The double form *C. palustris* 'Flore Pleno' is even finer and, although shorter and more compact, creates a dazzling display with fully double blooms like small pompon chrysanthemums. The white marsh marigold, *C. palustris* var. *alba*, is often catalogued by nurserymen, but is a mildew-prone plant with paltry off-white blooms of little significance. The mountain marigold, *C. leptosepala*, is a much better proposition with broad white blossoms of thick silky texture, held above foliage of the deepest green. A variety of this, *C.l.* var. *grandiflora* has even larger blooms and handsome foliage of corresponding magnitude. However, this is not the most substantial member of the family, for the Himalayan marsh marigold, *C. polypetala*, has dark green leaves up to 23 cm (9 in) across and huge trusses of golden yellow flowers on stems 90 cm (3 ft) high. All the calthas are extremely tolerant of situation, growing equally well in wet soil or several centimetres of water, but being more tidy and attractive under drier conditions.

■ *Skunk cabbages*

The skunk cabbages are also invaluable plants for enhancing the poolside in spring. With arum-like spathes of yellow or white, they provoke startled looks from visitors encountering them for the first time, for their glossy blooms are produced in advance of their foliage. The leaves, when they arrive, are large and leathery with a waxy surface, around which water globules bob and bounce like quick-silver. The American skunk cabbage, *Lysichiton americanum*, is the most frequently grown and has spathes of purest gold, a splendid companion for the slightly smaller, white-flowering, Japanese species *L. camtschatcense*. A hybrid between the two with creamy-white spathes can be seen in Savill Gardens, Windsor, but as far as I know is not in general cultivation. Both of the natural species set seed readily. When this has ripened and becomes a jelly-like mass it can be sown in trays of damp soil where it will germinate freely. Established plants can be divided during early spring with a sharp knife, but take a full season to recover, while those raised from seed take up to four years to flower. Not all skunk cabbages are lysichitons, for the plant to which this unfortunate common name really alludes is the North American *Symplocarpus foetidus*. Every spring without fail it produces clumps of dark purple hooded spathes of indescribably objectionable odour, succeeded by upright, broadly heart-shaped leaves of a pleasant green hue. Like the lysichitons, it is an adaptable plant growing in just moist ground or a little water.

■ *Bog bean*

The bog or buck bean, *Menyanthes trifoliata*, is a similar proposition. With dark green trifoliate leaves, rather like those of a broad bean, and attractive pinkish or white fringed flowers, it makes a bold display during spring and early summer. Surprisingly the bog bean is closely related to the primrose, and those with a botanical turn of mind will be interested to learn that the tiny frilled flowers occur in both thrum-eyed and pin-eyed forms. Seed sets readily and numerous greenish-yellow pea-like pods form, but these are seldom utilized for propagation, the long scrambling rhizomes being chopped into sections, each with a latent bud and vestige of root attached, and planted in pots of wet soil. Although often recommended as a pond plant, menyanthes objects to deep water and only thrives in the shallows, or when allowed to colonize the mud at the water's edge.

■ *Cuckoo flower*

The cuckoo flower, *Cardamine pratensis*, is a true waterside perennial, a spring delight for boggy soil in sun or shade. It has close tufts of ferny foliage, surmounted by slender stems with crowded spikes of rosy-lilac flowers. The double cuckoo flower *C.p. flore plena* is even more showy with full double blossoms. Unlike the single kind, which is easily increased from seed, the double one must be propagated by division.

■ *Primulas*

The same applies to *Primula rosea* and the cultivar 'Delight'. The latter, especially, is a first class early-flowering waterside primula, but one that can only be reliably increased from division. This ensures consistency in colour and stature, which is not so evident in seed-raised plants of the species. The flowers of *P. rosea* vary from pale rose through to deep rose-red, the latter shades being the more desirable and very similar to 'Delight'. Rather like refined primroses, with smooth coppery-green leaves, they look lovely when associated with the bright yellow spathes of *Lysichiton americanum*. So do the drumstick primulas, *P. denticulata* and its various forms. These produce rounded heads of blue or lilac flowers on short stout stems. The variety *alba* is white, and *cachemiriana* has lilac–purple blooms and mealy foliage.

□ Flowers of summer □

■ *Irises*

There are many more colourful bog plants that flower in summer than in early spring. Of these the irises are unquestionably the most important. A personal favourite is the Japanese clematis-flowered iris, *Iris kaempferi*, an elegant tufted plant with broad grassy leaves, surmounted by large clematis-like blossoms which appear amidst the foliage like resplendent tropical butterflies at rest. The ordinary species has purple flowers, but numerous hybrids have been evolved so that now there are varieties available in almost every shade of lilac, mauve and purple, together with white, and combinations of all these colours. *Iris kaempferi* cultivars are loosely divided into three types but it is the Ise strain which is the most elegant. This originated many years ago in the Ise district of Japan and has flowers which are characterized by having three petals, or occasionally up to six, but never any more. Their falls hang gracefully and each

Foliage and form at the streamside. Even when not in flower, waterside iris make a significant contribution with their sword-like leaves.

petal overlaps at its base, while standards stand obliquely upwards.

The Higo strain may have nine or more petals and prominent stamens. True Higo fanciers have little time for the modern double kinds as they are said to hide the 'hearts' of the flowers, but for garden decoration these double forms are superb. The only drawback is that in some of the older varieties the flowers are so heavy, and the stems so weak, that they are spoiled by wind and rain. Originally Higo irises were grown as pot plants for indoor decoration when this was of no account. However, in recent years Japanese breeders have been making a concerted effort to rectify this fault with considerable success. Edo varieties do not have this problem, for they are the older kinds and ancestors of both the Ise and Higo strains. There are no particular guidelines as to what constitutes an Edo variety, but the majority resemble the wild *I. kaempferi* in some way, but are usually of an entirely different colouring. In fact most are still in the form that the celebrated Japanese breeder Sho-oh left them over 120 years ago. For waterside planting, a good mixture derived from Ise or Edo varieties is admirable. This is the seed commonly sold commercially as *I. kaempferi* hybrids and will yield a wide colour range which will seldom produce a disappointing plant. Sown in moist soil directly in the open ground during early and mid-autumn, plants can be produced that are ready for putting in their permanent quarters by the end of the following summer. If you fancy experimenting with the Higo strain, then it is more desirable to select named varieties. Unfortunately most Higo cultivars have unpronounceable Japanese names, which even when translated are not very meaningful, seldom giving any indication of the floral delights that await the cultivator, but reasonable uniformity is assured.

The same to a certain extent applies to *I. sibirica*. Of the same general aspect as *I. kaempferi*, this is more easily grown, not resenting an alkaline soil like that species. *Iris sibirica* itself is not particularly exciting, cultivars like the purple 'Caesar', sky-blue 'Perry's Blue' and the glistening white 'Snow Queen' being far superior. *Iris sanguinea* is very much like *I. sibirica*, but with shorter flowering stems and more substantial blossoms. Apart from being used in hybridizing, it is nowadays seldom encountered, its place being taken by *I. setosa*. Occurring in a wide range of forms, this is a handsome easily grown plant, with broad sword-like foliage and large deep blue or purplish flowers. It is somewhat shorter than *I. sanguinea* and of more robust habit. When the flowering season is over its leafy fans can be separated, or young plants raised quickly and easily from seed which is produced in abundance each year.

The delightful Chinese *I. bulleyana* has similar virtues and, although not quite so striking as *I. setosa*, displays a modest charm that beckons the iris lover. Its fountains of slender grassy foliage support neatly sculptured blossoms of deep lavender-blue that call to mind that other iris fancier's delight, *I. chrysographes*. Indeed, if it were not for the colour of flower and more rounded falls, *I. bulleyana* could well be considered a mere variant of *I. chrysographes*. This has blossoms of a rich velvety purple, clearly etched with a tracery of golden lines. In the variety *rubella* the ground colour is deep plum and in the forms variously distributed as 'Kew Black', 'Black Knight' or straightforward 'Black Form', a very dark maroon. All are easy to please and flower quite freely. The same goes for hybrids derived from *I. chrysographes* like 'Desert Dream' and 'Margot Holmes'. Both are outstanding, 'Desert Dream' having fawn flowers with a rosy infusion, while 'Margot Holmes' is an intense crimson–purple.

It is important not to neglect some of the taller moisture-loving irises, even though their usefulness is restricted in smaller modern gardens. *Iris ochroleuca* grows 1 m (3 ft 3 in) or more high and has handsome glaucous foliage and contrasting white and gold blossoms, while the equally robust *I. aurea* produces striking deep yellow flowers, but foliage that lacks the stiff architectural quality of its cousin. Both are vigorous growers, but not as rampant as our native yellow flag, *I. pseudacorus*. This has broad sword-like leaves and attractive seed capsules and is only really suited to a wild garden. For the bog or streamside it is best replaced by one of its improved forms, the double *I.p.* 'Flore Pleno', golden and green-leafed 'Variegata' or the unfortunately named, soft pure yellow flowered var. *bastardii*

Iris versicolor is the North American counterpart of the European yellow flag. A splendid fellow, it has violet blue flowers veined with purple, and a conspicuous patch of yellow on the falls. Its variety 'Kermesina' is even more lovely, the blooms being of a gorgeous deep plum shade with the same distinctive markings. It is sometimes muddled with *I. laevigata*, the blue iris of the paddy fields, which produces sky-blue flowers during early summer. Many cultivars are freely available, and even if of slightly dubious origin, enjoy much the same conditions as *I. laevigata*. *Iris laevigata* 'Alba' which is white, 'Monstrosa' or 'Colchesteri', violet and white, and 'Rose Queen' are the most outstanding, together with the handsome cream and green variegated foliage form with soft blue flowers, which is known variously as 'Elegantissima' and 'Variegata'. Although truly aquatic and commonly recommended for growing in water, *I. laevigata* and its cultivars are very versatile and will prosper equally in mud or very damp soil.

■ *Musk*

So do most of the musks or mimulus; indeed only one could be called a permanent perennial aquatic. This is the dainty blue-flowered *Mimulus ringens*, a delicate-looking plant with much branched slender stems with handsome narrow leaflets. Its relatives have an altogether different aspect, being less reliable, but amongst the most brash and colourful plants for waterside planting, especially *M. luteus* and the closely allied *M. guttatus*, scrambling short-lived perennials that delight in spreading amongst reeds and rushes at the water's edge. Both have bright yellow blossoms, those of *M. guttatus* being spotted with red, while *M. luteus* has flowers which are prominently blotched with reddish-purple. Together with *M. cupreus*, these are the parents of many excellent strains capable of producing large vividly-coloured blossoms throughout the summer. Amongst my favourites are the bright red 'Bonfire' and boldly spotted 'Queen's Prize' strains, although the modern hybrids 'Royal Velvet' and 'Yellow Velvet' have much to commend them.

Mimulus cupreus is a smaller and more restrained character with striking fiery red flowers. A stunning plant and the parent of 'Whitecroft Scarlet', probably the most outstanding mimulus of all. This little gem produces neat mats of bright green foliage from which short stems rise, clothed with hooded blossoms of vivid scarlet. An excellent plant for the smaller waterside feature. The only other red flowered mimulus that is at all comparable is the amiable Californian *M. cardinalis*. Although not reliably hardy in colder districts, this lovely plant with its soft grey-green pubescent foliage and striking blossoms is worth growing even if it is likely to be a temporary inhabitant of the bog garden. So too is the attractive soft lilac-pink *M. lewisii*. Both this and

M. cardinalis, although doubtfully hardy, can be easily perpetuated as rooted cuttings if given the protection of a cold frame during the winter.

■ Lobelias

The same is true of most of the perennial moisture-loving lobelias. Although hardy in most places, it is wise to afford some protection to a few young plants during the winter in case the permanent plantings do not reappear. *Lobelia cardinalis* and *L. fulgens* are the two best known species, and hybrids from crosses between these two have always been popular, although perhaps not so latterly as in pre-war years. *Lobelia cardinalis* in its true form has plain green leaves and vivid red flowers, although in several commercial seed–raised strains the foliage is of a distinct purple or bronze shade. Indeed, the closely related *L. fulgens*, with its beetroot-coloured stems and leaves, and bright red flowers, is often mistakenly sold as *L. cardinalis*. Hybrids such as 'Queen Victoria' with very attractive maroon foliage and red flowers, 'Huntsman', brilliant scarlet, and 'Mrs. Humbert', flesh pink, embrace the characteristics of both. *Lobelia* × *vedrariensis* is a handsome hybrid of uncertain origin, absolutely hardy, and with tall spires of violet flowers and pea-green foliage splashed and bordered with maroon. Like all lobelias it must have moisture and also appreciates shade when such is available. So does the smaller blue-flowered *L. syphilitica*, a robust perennial which in its white flowered form is excellent for brightening up a gloomy corner.

■ Primulas

The candelabra primulas are also useful in wet shade, although they will flourish equally well in full sun. These are the primulas which have large coarse leaves and tiered whorls of flowers in myriad colours. There are innumerable species and varieties, but the most widely grown are *P. bulleyana*, *P. beesiana* and *P. pulverulenta*. All flower during early summer, *P. bulleyana* producing bold whorls of bright orange blossoms on stout stems, 60 cm (2 ft) high, while *P. beesiana* is of similar stature with blooms of rosy-carmine. However, it is *P. pulverulenta* which I favour, for not only does it have striking deep red blossoms with conspicuous purple eyes, but flower stems that are densely coated with a white farina. A superb strain that comes evenly from seed is called 'Bartley'. This consists of colours that vary from pale flesh to rich peach and is quite outstanding. *Primula japonica* is another good red, together with its cultivars 'Millers Crimson' and 'Postford White'. Good companions for the pale orange *P. chungensis* and dwarf orange-red *P. cockburniana*, two reliable sorts that can be raised easily from seed and will flower the following year.

Primula florindae and *P. sikkimensis* look rather like cowslips – indeed the former is often referred to as the Himalayan cowslip – but unlike the European cowslip it grows to a height of 90 cm (3 ft) or more. *P. sikkimensis* is almost identical but much dwarfer, with soft yellow flowers that are deliciously fragrant. *P. microdonta alpicola* and its variety *violacea* are of similar habit with drooping blooms in pendant clusters, but are additionally dusted liberally with white or yellowish meal. The species is soft yellow, while its variety, as

Garden primulas and wild rushes intermingle happily in this informal planting arrangement. A happy association if managed carefully.

one might expect, is deep violet-mauve.

Primula waltonii has clustered flowers of deep port wine, and *P. helodoxa* stout stems bearing whorls of rich yellow blooms, but the most bizarre and remarkable primula is *P. viali*. Although often not long–lived, this striking character has flower spikes of red and lilac in shape and contrast like those of a small red hot poker.

■ *Meadowsweets*

For something more subtle we must turn to the meadowsweets. The common meadowsweet, *Filipendula ulmaria*, although much loved by country folk for its frothy heads of fragrant blossoms, is seldom grown in gardens, although there is no reason why it should not be considered. Its beautiful double form, *F.u. flore pleno*, and the golden-green foliage variety 'Aurea', are much sought after and add quiet contrast and delicious fragrance to the poolside or bog garden. *Filipendula kamtschatica* enjoys similar conditions, and with its huge spreading leaves and heavy heads of sweetly scented flowers is reminiscent of a giant meadowsweet. *F.c. elegantissima rosea* is of deepest rose, while *F.c. carnea* has cloudy heads of soft apple-blossom pink. The dropwort, *F. hexapetala*, tolerates much drier conditions and during mid-summer produces crowded heads of icy white blossoms above neatly rounded hummocks of fern-like foliage. As it rarely grows more than 60 cm (2 ft) high, it is ideal for the smaller water feature, while those who have a natural pool or large expanse of water should grow *F. rubra magnifica*, an immense plant with vine-like leaves and spreading masses of glistening peach-pink flowers up to 1.8 m (6 ft) high. All the filipendulas are easy-going in moist conditions and readily propagated from division or rooted pull-offs in early spring.

■ *Day lilies*

The hemerocallis or day lilies are amongst the most useful and colourful perennial plants for the bog garden, most revelling in really wet soil in full sun rather than in the drier conditions of the average herbaceous border. The diversity of material now available is enormous, many of the excellent new cultivars from North America superseding our traditional European varieties. A review of the best cultivars therefore becomes very difficult and subject to considerable personal prejudice. The best way of coping with such a situation is to suggest that any cultivars introduced from the mid 1960's, and those from former times which still appear in nurserymen's catalogues, are worthy of consideration. The earlier varieties that have survived will be weather resistant, with relatively large flowers, and more than the average number of flowers on a stem. This ensures a longer period of colour, for most hemerocallis blossoms wither in the evening of the day that they unfurl, and continuity of flowering is essential if the variety is to retain its place in the garden.

Modern day lily breeders have worked on this problem and now most new cultivars have greater numbers of blossoms and scapes that are more evenly branched. This latter ensures that the flowers are not all crowded together at the summit of the panicles. Varieties with flat open flowers, often with ruffled petals, have replaced the funnel-shaped cultivars of earlier years and it is now possible to obtain dwarf kinds and varieties with more or less evergreen foliage. Indeed the diversity of forms and wide range of habits exhibited by modern day lilies are legion. Sadly, one aspect seems to have been neglected and that is fragrance. Some breeders have endeavoured to retain it, but size, colour and length of flowering period tend to have overridden this most important characteristic. This is why I believe we ought to bring back some of the species and, if possible, rescue some of the early cultivars.

The old-fashioned *Hemerocallis lilio-asphodelus*, probably better known as *H. flava*, is the most important early cultivar. A widely distributed native of northern Europe and much of Asia, it flowers during late spring and early summer with branched panicles of clear yellow scented blossoms. These are funnel-shaped and borne in profusion on slender wiry stems which emanate from neat tufts of bright green foliage. Together with *H. citrina*, which is also richly fragrant, it makes a duo that for elegance and simplicity are unsurpassed by any of the modern cultivars. As might be expected, *H. citrina* has flowers of citron-yellow in panicles 1 m (3 ft 3 in) or so high. The individual blooms are an open funnel-shape and produced continuously during summer time. Unlike most day lilies these unfurl during late afternoon and expire at noon the following day. *Hemerocallis fulva* is of similar habit, and at first glance may be taken as just an orange form of *H. citrina*. However, closer inspection will reveal that the petals are blunt and much broader, often with crinkled margins, and the flowers carried in shorter panicles above not unattractive, but coarser foliage. Probably few nurserymen will be willing to reintroduce this species as it has a reputation for being invasive. Despite this, many of its forms are worthy garden plants, and a determined effort could see their revival, for all are easily and quickly increased by division.

Hemerocallis fulva var. *maculata* is like an improved version of the species, with larger flowers of a different shape and with darker internal zoning, while *H. fulva* var. *rosea* is a trifle smaller with delightful blossoms in pink or red. These are in marked contrast to *H. fulva* var. *longituba*, in which the flower tube is elongated and of brilliant jaffa orange. However, for something really different we have to turn to the double *H. fulva* var. *kwanso*. A native of Japan, this has lovely orange double blossoms and plain green tussocks of foliage. Unfortunately, it is often confused with the somewhat bizarre *H. fulva* var. *kwanso foliis variegatis*, a form with irregularly striped cream and white leaves and curious orange-red flowers filled with a central tuft of small petal-like segments. The latter is more a curiosity than a beauty, but its progenitor is worthy of attention.

Hemerocallis aurantiaca is a most attractive species with trumpet-shaped flowers of deep orange on erect stems 1 m (3 ft 3 in) or more high. Its foliage is interesting, for unlike many other day lilies it remains more or less evergreen, certainly persisting well into the new year. A more vigorous form, *H. aurantiaca major*, is sometimes encountered, but there is speculation as to whether this is in fact a variation of *H. aurantiaca* or a chance seedling from an accidental cross. Mention of hybridizing brings to mind *H. forrestii*, for this delightful fellow has been widely used in breeding and has contributed considerably in the quest for shorter and more compact day lilies. When first given a plant of this I was unimpressed, for its foliage is slender, almost grass-like and very ordinary. However, my views were drastically revised the following summer when it erupted into a fountain of brilliant yellow. A truly lovely plant.

■ *Apache beads*

So too is the North American apache beads, *Anemopsis californica*. Although not always considered as reliably hardy, it is still well worth acquiring. It looks rather like an herbaceous anemone, but with flowers that consist of a hard

central cone surrounded by a single whorl of pearly-white petal-like bracts. Only in damp mud or shallow water with an alkaline tendency is this little fellow really at home, but then he will grow with great gusto forming sizeable clumps that can be readily divided. The roots have an overpowering sickly fragrance and were used for medicinal purposes in former years. So were the leaves and roots of the hedge hyssop, *Gratiola officinalis*, and several of the other lesser known gratiola species. The common *G. officinalis* is an interesting bog plant for the larger garden, sporting delicate serrated foliage and small, pretty blue flowers, but most of the others are rather mundane.

■ *Astilbes*

That is something that could never be attributed to the astilbes or false goat's beard. All members of this attractive family flourish in a moist situation in sun or shade and produce clumps of handsome pale green foliage surmounted by dense feathery spikes of flowers. The popular hybrids of today are the result of unions between various Asiatic species such as *A. astilboides*, *A. japonica*, *A. sinensis* and *A. thunbergii*. None of these are encountered in cultivation as

Above: *Tangled informality in the bog garden. Native rushes and ferns shoulder to shoulder with brightly coloured primulas.*
Opposite: *Bold drifts of early summer-flowering Harlow Car Hybrid primulas, the finest mixed strain for waterside planting.*

they produce relatively sparse and untidy flower spikes, but the hybrids that they have yielded are numerous and include 'Fanal' which is bright crimson, 'White Gloria' and the delicious salmon-pink 'Peach Blossom'. These and any of the other widely commercialized varieties make bold splashes of colour when planted in groups of six or eight and if one is to study any reputable grower's catalogue, suitable varieties combining the desired heights and colours can easily be selected.

For the gardener with a very tiny bog garden there are two varieties of a dwarf stature. These are the *Astilbe crispa* cultivars 'Lilliput' and 'Perkeo'. Both have congested tufts of dark crinkled foliage, the former producing spires of tightly packed salmon–pink flowers and the latter blooms of an intense deep pink and neither exceeding a height of 15 cm (6 in) even under ideal conditions. A slightly taller kind which generally reaches 30 cm (1 ft) or so in height, *A. chinensis pumila*, has prostrate tufts of dark green foliage from which stout spikes of rosy-purple flowers are produced.

■ *Goat's beards*

The true goat's beards are the aruncus, the most important being *Aruncus sylvester*, or as the botanists now call it, *A. dioicus*. A tall handsome plant of astilbe-like appearance, it carries waving plumes of creamy-white flowers above pale green deeply-cut leaves that are produced on stout bamboo-like stems. A dwarf cultivar called 'Kneiffii', is better suited to the smaller garden, having all the virtues of the species, but rarely growing more than 90 cm (3 ft) high.

■ *Loosestrife*

I like to see the purple loosestrifes growing in association with aruncus. There are only two species commonly cultivated, but both, together with their myriad cultivars, are well worth acquiring. *Lythrum salicaria* is the plant that most gardeners refer to as purple loosestrife. This has stiff bushy stems and spires of flowers some 1.2 m (4 ft) high. Improved garden varieties include 'The Beacon', 'Lady Sackville', and 'Robert' which cover the range from purple through rose-red to pink, 'Robert' being especially useful as it has a neat, compact habit. *Lythrum virgatum* is an altogether smaller character, but nonetheless effective, particularly in a confined space. It has dark green leaves and purple flowers on stems 75 cm (2 ft 6 in) in height. Named varieties derived from *L. virgatum* are less inspiring than those from its more vigorous cousin, but 'Rose Queen' and 'Dropmore Purple' are well worth considering.

Yellow loosestrife, *Lysimachia punctata*, is a different species of a different genus, but nevertheless a very welcome addition to the bog garden. It has bright yellow buttercup-like flowers borne in clusters on stout upright stems. These attain a height of 60 cm (2 ft) or so and are heavily clothed with dense whorls of ovate leaves. A native of eastern Europe and Asia Minor, it grows in any damp place, even the most difficult and gloomy of corners being lightened by its presence. These virtues are to be discovered in *L. clethroides* too, a lusty character with bold green foliage and late summer or early autumn racemes of small white flowers.

■ *Ligularia*

The garden groundsels flower at around the same time. Yes, these are close relatives of that small troublesome weed, but remain well behaved plants for the modern garden. They were formerly called senecio, but now rest easily with the name *Ligularia*. All are herbaceous, moisture-loving, and with broad, roughly heart-shaped leaves and huge mop heads, or else erect spikes of droopy orange or yellow daisy-like flowers. In a moist situation they are magnificent, but they must be kept permanently damp or else they wilt badly and become stunted and weedy.

The best-loved species is undoubtedly *Ligularia clivorum*, with broad leaves and strong branching stems of bright orange flowers some 1.2 m (4 ft) high. With its improved cultivar forms, such as the vivid 'Orange Queen', pale yellow-flowered and purple-leafed 'Desdemona', and purplish-leafed 'Othello', it makes a brave show during late summer. For the smaller garden there is 'Gregynog Gold' with bright golden flowers and of diminutive stature.

Unfortunately, *L. clivorum* and its varieties hybridize and seed very freely, producing colonies of young plants with attractive foliage but, if allowed to develop, they form plants with straggly stems and mediocre flowers. The best policy with all ligularia seedlings is to hoe them out immediately they are seen. Apart from *L. clivorum* there are several other species which produce spikes of flowers rather than mop heads. These flower during late summer and are particularly attractive when grouped with cultivars of *L. clivorum*. *Ligularia hessei* grows up to 1.8 m (6 ft) high with spikes of glowing orange, while *L. veitchiana* has heart-shaped leaves and blooms of golden yellow.

■ *Monkshood*

The common monkshood, *Aconitum napellus*, is perhaps surprisingly a bog plant. While it is true that this and many other varieties of aconitum can be grown in the ordinary border, it is also true to say that the blooms and foliage produced there pale into insignificance when compared with the magnificence of plants grown under conditions of continuous moisture. The common monkshood has tall, erect spikes of hooded navy-blue flowers about 1.5 m (5 ft) high. They are somewhat delphinium-like in appearance, as is the bright green, rounded foliage. Apart from the common kind there is a blue and white bi-coloured form called *A.n. bicolor*, and a dwarf, stocky, deep blue variety which seldom exceeds 60 cm (2 ft) in height called 'Bressingham Spire'. *Aconitum wilsonii* and its cultivar 'Barker's Variety' are a complete contrast, growing 1.5 m (5 ft) high and flowering in early autumn, at least three months after their cousins. *Aconitum lycoctonum* is unusual in so far as it has yellow flowers, but the best form is var. *pyrenaicum*, a compact fellow with large hooded flowers. However, the real surprise amongst the monkshoods is the climbing species *A. volubile*. If given a twiggy support or small shrub amidst which to scramble, this gangling character makes a brave and exciting show.

■ *Anemone*

There are two species of anemone that can be grown successfully in the bog garden; indeed *A. virginiana* can even stand periodic flooding. If left to its own devices it soon forms clumps of hairy leaves on 90 cm (3 ft) stems and bears clusters of greenish-white flowers throughout the summer. Its relative *A. rivularis* is much finer, with loose umbels of snow-white flowers which have central clusters of prominent violet anthers.

■ *Spearworts*

Rather surprisingly the spearworts belong to the same family as the anemones. These are moisture-loving versions of the buttercups, some of which are popularly grown as marginal aquatics, but which will also prosper in the wet soil conditions of a bog garden. *Ranunculus lingua*, the greater spearwort, is the largest species. It has erect hollow stems well clothed with narrow dark-green leaves and produces golden flowers in abundance throughout the summer. A natural octoploid variant, *R. lingua* 'Grandiflora', is the plant commonly sold by nurseries and is an even larger and finer subject. If you have a limited amount of space the diminutive *R. flammula* or lesser spearwort is more appropriate. Like a superior buttercup, it bears glistening golden blooms above dark-green oval leaves and slender reddish stems which, in the varieties *R. flammula* var. *tenuifolius* and *R. flammula* subsp. *scoticus*, scramble across damp soil or mud rooting at every leaf joint. All the bog garden and marginal spearworts are most attractive, but they need siting carefully as they rapidly outgrow their allotted space.

■ *Other bog plants*

This is not the case with the North American pickerel weed, *Pontederia cordata*, for this choice and well behaved marginal aquatic spreads quite slowly. Preferring to grow in a little standing water at the poolside, pontederia produces several stems, each consisting of an oval or lance-shaped shiny green leaf and a leafy bract from which the spike of soft blue flowers emerges. In wet soil conditions the plants become stocky and have a more solid look about them (in much the same way as marsh marigolds). So does the lovely pink flowered *Butomus umbellatus* or flowering rush. This associates with pontederia like love with marriage, a perfect complement with narrow triquetrous foliage and bold umbels of rose-pink flowers. It also seems to flower more regularly and with many more umbels than when growing in water, but I have to admit that foliage quality is not so good when butomus is grown in the bog garden. Under such conditions there tends to be a proliferation of bulbils at the base of the plants and these give rise to finer grassy foliage. When this occurs, regular lifting of the plants so that bulbils can be removed is useful, not only to produce plants of more presentable appearance, but to increase stock, for each bulbil is a potential new plant.

The swamp milkweed, *Asclepias incarnata*, is a splendid subject for moist areas near a natural pond or streamside. Its only requirements are sunshine and abundant moisture and then it will produce stout leafy stems and crowded heads of rose-coloured flowers. Apart from the ordinary variety, there is a kind with white flowers called *A.i.* var. *alba*. Then there are the eupatoriums, a useful genus of strong-growing perennials forming bold bushes of dark-green foliage with crowded heads of flowers that are particularly useful for the larger bog garden or streamside planting. *Eupatorium ageratoides* or *E. fraseri*, as it is more often known, has dense heads of white flowers on 60 cm (2 ft) high stems, as does the slightly bolder *E. perfoliatum*. *Eupatorium cannabinum* is the variety with plum-coloured blooms in large terminal heads and *E. purpureum* the tallest of all, sporting crowded heads of purple flowers.

For the smaller bog garden there are a number of short-growing plants that can be utilized, amongst them the tiny bog asphodel, *Narthecium ossifragum*. This is a little plant with a wiry creeping rootstock and small fans of reddish-

The bold architectural foliage of the ornamental rhubarb adds an exotic touch to this shaded streamside.

green iris-like foliage among which terminal racemes of bright yellow flowers are produced. Although a useful plant for the bog garden, it cannot be unreservedly recommended for the margins of a pool or streamside as it does not seem to tolerate any permanent significant depth of water over the crown.

The same applies to the swamp aster, *Aster puniceus*. A most interesting and useful plant, it will stand very wet conditions, but not those of permanent immersion, especially during the winter months. With rigid red stems 90 cm (3 ft) high, it is for the moderately sized water feature, rather than the tiny bog garden. A billowing plant with clouds of small lilac-coloured blossoms and soft green foliage.

If you are seeking the ultimate in bog plants you need look no further than the grass of Parnassus, *Parnassia palustris*. A really choice plant, this has heart-shaped leaves and slender stems bearing snow-white flowers, occasionally blotched with apple-green. It grows best in a damp peaty soil, preferably close to moving water such as a stream or cascade. A plant to test the gardener's skill, it is very difficult to cultivate, but when treated properly and happily established it is an absolute joy. The 'crème de la crème' among bog plants.

At the other end of the scale there is the starfruit, *Damasonium alisma*, a plant of relatively little horticultural merit, but one of which I am very fond and would always include in my bog garden. Its flower spikes are stout and upright with whorls of milky-white blooms which are followed by curious star-shaped fruits full of viable seed. The leaves are strap shaped and arise from a hard corm-like rootstock which in large plants will divide for propagation purposes.

Bupthalmum salicifolium is another plant of questionable merit, but one which I always accommodate if I have the room. It is sometimes grown in the herbaceous border, but grows so much better in the bog garden with spreading hummocks of yellow daisy-like flowers. There is a bigger, swamp species called *B. speciosum* and this has hairy aromatic foliage and large, drooping yellow daisy-like flowers.

Finally, among the summer flowering bog garden plants I must commend the anthericums, a lovely genus of summer flowering perennials with tufts of narrow grassy foliage from which arise numerous slender spikes of pure white flowers. *Anthericum liliago* is the St. Bernard's lily, and the most readily obtainable. It possesses grassy foliage and 60 cm (2 ft) high spikes of white flowers.

□ Shrubby swamp lovers □

Apart from the many plants of herbaceous character that enjoy life in the bog garden, there are a number of shrubby fellows of considerable merit that deserve a place. If carefully planted not only can they provide a permanent structural thread through the feature, but winter interest too. Observation of the flowering periods of bog plants reveals the virtual non-existence of plants with winter interest. Fortunately most of the shrubby swamp lovers have important autumnal or winter characteristics and it is for these which the majority are planted in other parts of the garden.

The dogwoods and willows which are grown for their coloured stems offer the greatest diversity, the red stemmed *Cornus alba* 'Sibirica' being the most outstanding of all. 'Elegantissima' does not have such brightly coloured stems, but provides a bonus of cream and green variegated foliage during the summer months. Yellow stems are provided by *C. stolonifera* 'Flaviramea', while we have to turn to willows like *Salix alba* 'Chermesina' for orange shoots and the violet willow, *S. daphnoides*, for those of a purple hue. All these coloured-stem shrubs derive from a system of cultivation called stooling. This is the selecting of suitable forms and cultivars which have produced brightly coloured shoots the previous summer. Regularly cutting such plants to the ground each spring ensures that all the new growth is only a season old and therefore brightly coloured.

Stooled shrubs like this have many virtues and not least that the curtailment of their size by constant pruning leaves room for other swamp-living woody plants which tend to be quite vigorous and can soon outgrow their position. This is particularly true of willows that are not stooled, especially the lovely, but generally unmanageable weeping willow, *S. babylonica*. A native of China and long cultivated in Britain, it is this tree which was once widely planted along river banks to good effect. In the small or medium-sized garden it is over-bearing, smothering nearby plants and disrupting the garden with its probing roots. It is not a good poolside tree as its fallen leaves not only pollute the water by decomposing, but as they contain a toxin akin to aspirin, usually succeed in killing the fish too. As a riverside tree with plenty of room they are fine, especially beside a river that flows swiftly and quickly washes away fallen leaves. If you have a situation where a weeping willow is a must – and I find such a situation difficult to imagine – then choose the golden-yellow *S.* × *chrysocoma*, a hybrid of lasting, elegant beauty.

Amongst the willows of modest proportions is our native woolly willow, *S. lanata*, a great grey mound of foliage bedecked during early spring with golden candle-like catkins. An amenable character, it can be cut back quite severely if you think that it is getting out of hand. The same applies to the creeping willow, *S. repens*, a scrambling shrub of no great distinction, but one which can equally disguise the harsh edge of a water feature or prevent soil erosion on a muddy bank.

■ *Blueberries*

The blueberries are tremendous assets if you have an acid soil. Not only are there the popular fruiting kinds but many with attractive autumn colouring too. Indeed, most have both, especially the popular highbush blueberry, *Vaccinium corymbosum*, and its various commercial selections. These named selections are vegetatively propagated, very uniform in every respect, and have been developed for fruit production. In view of this, I much prefer to introduce the ordinary species, with all its variation, into the decorative garden. There is diversity in stature, leaf colour and both flowering and fruiting, and it is this that I think lends charm to an ornamental planting. The flowers of the highbush blueberry are rather small and not unlike those of lily of the valley, but its fruits are not only edible, but most decorative, being almost black with a distinctive blue bloom. These are borne in profusion amongst foliage, which at the approach of autumn, changes colour from green and copper to scarlet and wine.

The low bush blueberry, *V. angustifolium*, is a dwarfer kind with wiry branches and handsome foliage which turns fiery in the autumn. Its flowers are cylindrical or bell-shaped, white tinged with red, and followed in the autumn by blue-black fruits which are good to eat. Unfortunately those of the farkle-berry, *V. arboreum*, are not edible at all, but the shrub is most decorative and revels in damp acid soil. It produces pendant white bell-like flowers, often in

Above: *Although liberally planted with moisture-loving plants, there is still provision for the manicured lawn to reach down to the water.*
Opposite: *Most waterside primulas will tumble happily from the bank into the water. In favourable conditions they will seed themselves freely.*

clusters, and black fruits which hang amidst leathery foliage that has rich autumn tints.

■ *Swamp cypress*

Autumn colour is the main virtue of the swamp cypress, *Taxodium distichum*, a deciduous conifer and one of the finest for wet places. In the spring this irregular, pyramidal tree is clothed in bright green which mellows in the summer and then turns to coppery-amber as the first frosts arrive. An extraordinary character, this is the only hardy tree that I know of that in very wet conditions provides itself with a means of 'breathing' from the roots. With maturity, large knobbly lumps, scientifically called pneumatophores, appear above soil and water level to gasp at the air. Rather inappropriately these are called 'knees', but they are an added curious and unusual characteristic to the many that make taxodium well worth growing.

CHAPTER THREE

STREAM AND POOLSIDE

Apart from the bog garden alone, there are the associations of bog garden and pool, as well as the stream and poolside. All have water in common and many can successfully accommodate the same plants, but the problems with each are wide and varied. Some are common to all; many are peculiar to one. Special consideration must be afforded to each feature.

□ Preparing the streamside □

Few gardeners are fortunate enough to have a natural stream, but when there is such a marvellous feature available, then it should be used to provide an important focus in the garden. Remember though, that a natural stream or rill is just passing through, it is not exclusively yours, so it is unwise to interfere unduly with it. This is particularly true if it is of minor local importance, for interfering with its flow in the most innocent of ways may lead to the inadvertent flooding of your property, or that of a neighbour's, with the consequent strained relations.

■ Diverting flow of a stream

The only safe way in which the flow of a stream may be checked or diverted is by the addition of stepping stones. Strategically placed, these can create a calm area near either bank in which aquatic plants may be more successfully grown than out in mid-stream.

Where a stream is wide or deep a bridge may be necessary to enable it to be crossed, or even when this is not essential, a well constructed bridge can be introduced as an important visual feature. Stepping stones can also be used, but where these are intended to be used as a means of crossing the water, rather than diverting it, it is vital that the surface of each is smooth but not slippery, and of sufficient size to accommodate a large foot.

When suitable local stone is available, then this should be used, but avoid limestone as it erodes quite quickly. Also sandstone, for this is badly shaled by frost. If suitable stone is difficult to come by, then it is possible to make your own stepping stones easily and cheaply by mixing one part by volume of cement to three parts by volume of aggregate and pouring this into holes dug in the ground the size and shape of the desired stones. When the 'stones' have set, they can be excavated and placed in position. Within a few weeks they will start to take on a weathered appearance.

Fig. 4 *Dealing with erosion of bank.*

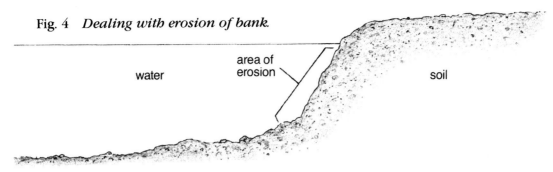

(a) Fast-flowing or turbulent streams quickly cause bank erosion, even when planted.

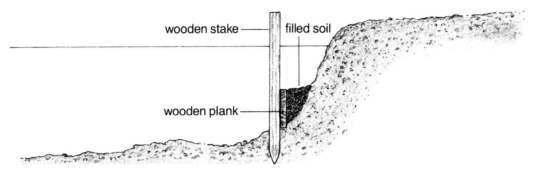

(b) Stakes firmly hammered into the stream bed at the base of the eroded bank provide support for protective planking.

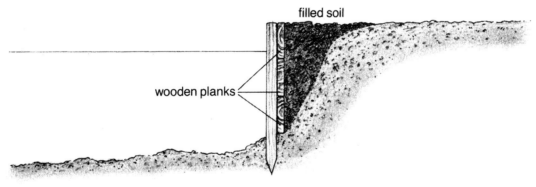

(c) As each plank is put in place, fill with soil to trap it against its support. Continue until above maximum water level.

■ Coping with erosion

Whether or not you decide to alter the flow of your stream, in the course of a year certain parts of the bank will tend to erode, particularly where there is no plant cover. This happens most frequently during the winter months when the water level rises quickly and the rate of water flow can increase alarmingly. This is particularly common before or after a bend, for it tends to divert the current's main flow from the centre and leads to erosion by scouring or by undermining the base of the bank so that the top subsides. Sheet erosion of the top soil also occurs near bends and has to be combated artificially.

Several kinds of options are open to the gardener when merely planting the affected area is not sufficient (Fig. 4). Wood and steel are the most frequently used materials. Never use concrete. This is an uncompromising material that is rigid and incapable of satisfactorily withstanding the often opposing pressures of soil and water. It is also extremely difficult to disguise. Wood is the easiest material to work with and the most pleasing to the eye. The clever gardener can often, by driving stakes and erecting boards in the water close by the mud, reclaim an area of rich alluvial silt, which if mixed with a little regular garden soil provides a first class medium for the cultivation of moisture-loving plants.

Moisture-loving is the key word, for a stream, while being a lovely feature during the summer, can turn into a raging horror during the winter, particularly after a thaw, when plants may become submerged for several days at a time. It is also wise to consider the proximity of your garden to the coast, for a stream that leads into a brackish river can itself become brackish at high tide, causing irreparable damage to some plants.

■ Preparing to plant

Dealing with primary erosion is one thing, cultivating stream banks and coping with the increased potential for such problems is quite another. Immediately you start to cultivate the soil, erosion begins, unless you are very cunning. Before they are gardened, most streamsides have a covering of native flora. These plants hold the banks together and prevent the soil being displaced. So initially the idea should be to kill the plant growth, but allow the old roots to bind the bank together.

Use a systemic herbicide so that all the plant tissue is killed, but only the weed top growth collapses, thereby allowing it to decompose back into the soil. Once this process has started, go across the surface of the sprayed area with a generous mulch of well rotted animal manure or garden compost. This smothers any seedling weeds and during the course of the summer decomposes and forms a rich organic medium for planting. This surface medium comprises the mulch and the decomposed remains of the original weedcover, but at the same time the old roots of that growth are still binding the banks together. Providing that planting takes place during the winter or spring following the destruction of the weed-cover, then the streamside plants will take over the role of erosion prevention from the slowly dying weed.

■ Choosing grass

Of course, as gardeners we tend to think of the streamside as having to be planted with brightly coloured marsh plants, but this is not always desirable. A green grassy sward sweeping down to a sparkling stream can be just as beautiful. Achieving such simplicity is not quite so easy, for minimal cultivation without the addition of an excessive amount of organic matter is necessary, especially if the sward is to be established from seed.

Whether it be seed or turf, the banks must be cultivated, light forking of the weed-free area being a minimum requirement. However, this can lead to erosion or collapse of certain areas and therefore stabilizing is necessary. Landscape contractors are able to purchase a fine weave matting to peg to vulnerable areas, which allows grass to grow through, but the home gardener

This rock stream provides a home for yellow mimulus and myriad primulas.

has to depend upon fine garden netting. The kind used for windbreaks is quite suitable, the material being pegged firmly to the soil from below minimum water level to above expected high water level. Turf can then be laid over the top, or compost scattered over the netting and seeds sown into this.

■ *Grass varieties*

When choosing to sow grass seed on a streamside banking, it is important that you choose a mixture that is suitable for the purpose. Just as there are myriad decorative plant varieties, so too are there many grass varieties.

If the bank is going to take a lot of foot traffic, then a hard-wearing mixture containing rye grass should be used. This is a coarse grass, but remains green, even during times of adversity. Some gardeners have a reluctance to include it in a mixture, believing that they will always be troubled by those coarse spiky shoots which are difficult to cut with a cylinder mower. Modern rye grass varieties are much improved and this problem rarely arises. An alternative for rye grass is the smooth stalked meadow grass. Of similar habit, this cannot be cut as short as perennial rye. It is particularly useful, though, if any of the bank is shaded, or if you have an area planted with spring flowering bulbs where the grass can be allowed to grow a little longer.

These two species are rarely included in the same mixture. The other components are usually Chewing's fescue, creeping red fescue and browntop bent. The Chewing's fescue should be the dominant species in a hard wearing sward, while the creeping red fescue will feature more strongly where shade is likely to be a problem. Banking that is intended to provide a pleasant background for rippling waters should be composed of fine lawn grasses, including Chewing's fescue, creeping red fescue and browntop bent in varying proportions. Creeping bent and velvet bent are fine grasses that can also be considered, but only where soil conditions are good. Neither will tolerate adversity, especially constant flooding. Creeping bent is especially troubled by wet conditions, but will not prosper in summer drought either. However, when it is well managed, it is a first class constituent of a decorative grass mixture, giving a distinctive spongy feel to the turf.

□ Poolside problems □

In an earlier chapter I outlined the difficulties and methods of integrating a bog garden with a pool. The success of this depends very much upon early planning, although it is possible to place a bog garden adjacent to a pool without a physical link if the bog feature is considered after pool construction. Or if you inherit a pool and then want a marshy area nearby. As described earlier, this is contrived as a shallow basin made out of either a pool liner or concrete. Each creates suitable conditions within, but what about the soil just outside?

■ *Dry soil*

For the most part this is going to be at least as dry as the soil in the rest of the garden, although in the immediate vicinity of a concrete surround it may be very shallow and consequently dust dry, especially when exposed to full sun. Soil and plants are the finest combination for disguising harsh edges and the best must be made of the two in every situation. Consequently careful selection of suitable plant material is vital, together with the incorporation of fairly liberal quantities of organic matter in order to conserve as much moisture as possible. Even then, the soil around a concrete lip may not be deep enough to accommodate anything but the least appropriate alpine subject, so a little cunning has to be employed. Instead of growing plants directly into the shallow soil where they will have difficulty in becoming established, plant them in the nearest position where they can obtain a full root run. If you select only creeping plants like *Lysimachia nummularia*, then the trailing shoots can be positioned across the soil and allowed to root wherever the joints touch the soil. This helps to establish a fixed vegetative sward, but the plant cover still has a life-line back to established roots if times become hard.

This technique can be adapted for marginal aquatic subjects too, for it is often easier to obtain good camouflage from plants within the pond, rather than from those outside. Well established marginal plants like common brooklime, *Veronica beccabunga*, and water mint, *Mentha aquatica*, delight in scrambling out of the water and into soil, surviving surprisingly harsh conditions when maintaining an umbilical cord into the water. Once such plant cover has been established, conditions immediately outside the pool start to improve, for the sun does not dry the soil out so rapidly.

Annuals and other seed-raised plants are often easier to establish in the harsh outer conditions around a pool if sown *in situ*. Unless the feature is very formal, or depending for its success upon colour rather than the cool tranquillity of the water, then most modern hardy annuals are unsuited. In the main they are very garish and do not lend themselves to a feature which most gardeners consider should be one of cool reflectiveness. A number of scrambling annuals, notably the charming little convolvulus, are well suited to such a situation, not announcing their presence in a loud fashion, but modestly hiding the undesirable and presenting a pleasing floral display. Amongst hardy and half hardy annuals there are a number of useful sorts, including mixed candytuft, the poached egg plant *Limnanthes douglasii*, *Sanvitalia procumbens* and Livingstone daisies.

■ *Ground cover plants*
At the moment only the close environs of the pool with shallow soil have been considered, but for at least a part of the edge there is likely to be an opportunity to establish deeper rooted, more permanent plants, especially some of those referred to popularly as ground cover. A number are traditionally offered as shade dwelling subjects, but all will respond to an open sunny position as well, and by virtue of their carpeting habit are by and large perfect for closing the gap between pool edge and garden.

PERIWINKLES   Periwinkles are amongst the best of these, carpeting the ground in sprawling evergreen foliage which during midsummer twinkles with starry blossoms. In the lesser periwinkle, *Vinca minor*, they are 2 or 3 cm across, bright blue, and produced in the axils of the leaves, while the greater periwinkle, *V. major*, sports much larger flowers amongst more substantial foliage. Both have variegated forms, and *V. minor* has white, purple, and double flowered varieties too. Each roots at the tips of extension growths, but *V. minor* will root at leaf joints as well, making an impenetrable mass.

The rose of Sharon, *Hypericum calycinum*, is another first class evergreen ground cover subject for harsh conditions. Throughout the summer its handsome foliage is littered with bright golden blossoms up to 10 cm (4 in)

across. In a situation to its liking, this hypericum can make itself a nuisance and may need controlling. *Hypericum moseranum* is a more orderly, slightly taller hybrid with smaller flowers with conspicuous orange-red anthers.

THYMES   If you have a dry open area that requires carpeting, then few plants can surpass the hairy, grey-leafed *Thymus lanuginosus*. Apart from being tough and aromatic, it produces a flush of tiny pink blossoms each summer which are irresistible to bees. The wild shepherd's thyme, *T. serpyllum*, can be used in the same way, but rarely makes such an impenetrable mat. This has dark green, glossy leaves and myriad deep pink blossoms which will hang over the pool edge and down to the water like a delicate jewelled curtain.

VIOLAS   Some of the violas are useful for poolside planting, especially those that we regard as violets. The sweet violet, *Viola odorata*, can be used with reasonable effect, but the deep purple-leafed *V. labradorica* is the most successful and beautiful of all. The larger flowered kinds can also be utilized, *V. cornuta* and its various forms being the best. The species has lovely clear green foliage and light blue flowers with just a hint of purple, while the variety *alba* is a cool icy white. Unlike many violas, the cornuta types are persistent perennials, only occasionally needing replacement from soft summer cuttings which root readily in an equal parts mixture of peat and sharp sand.

CRANESBILLS   Many of the geraniums or cranesbills are excellent for disguising an unyielding pool edge, tolerating a wide range of soil conditions and producing a diversity of form and colour. *Geranium endressii* 'Wargrave Pink' seldom grows more than 45 cm (1 ft 6 in) high and is extremely useful. So too is the blue-flowered *G. platypetalum* and the taller magenta *G. psilostemon*. All flower during the summer and are beautiful when reflected in water.

EPIMEDIUMS   Epimediums bloom a little earlier, but it is not their blossoms that are the main attraction: it is for their outstanding foliage that these dwarf relatives of the berberis are cultivated. Innumerable kinds are available, but *Epimedium warleyense*, with coppery flowers, and the yellow-flowered *E. grandiflorum* are among the most popular, although *E. pinnatum colchicum* should be considered for its vivid red autumn colour. All epimediums are semi-evergreen and tolerate a wide range of soil conditions, prospering in either sun or shade.

DEADNETTLES   The various lamiums or dead nettles are useful for hostile situations, cultivars of the yellow flowered *Lamium galeobdolon* and purple-flowering *L. maculatum* being especially resilient. Lamiums should only be considered for harsh conditions on poor soils where they are unlikely to become invasive and the colours of the variegated kinds will be enhanced. Excellent plants for difficult places. However, if you have to resort to these, then you have certainly got problems, and it may be that consideration should be given to altering part of the pool structure, or even using paving or other hard landscaping material instead.

A pool framed with shrubs, ferns and variegated water grass provides a glassy vista into the main garden.

CHAPTER FOUR

PLANTS FOR STREAM AND POOLSIDE

There is a greater diversity of plants available for stream and poolside planting than there is for the bog garden. Not only can moisture-loving plants be accommodated, but those that require ordinary garden conditions too. The poolside is not always damp; indeed it is often dry alongside an artificially contrived pool, yet plants of an appropriate character are desired. Similarly with a stream, the plants have to be adaptable, for few streams have a constant level of water. Fluctuations lead to either permanently wet, occasionally wet, or constantly dry soil conditions, yet as with the poolside, the streamside must have plants appropriate to the setting. Within those that are visually appealing it is essential to select suitable kinds for the soil conditions which prevail. The prudent gardener faced with choosing suitable plants will certainly depend heavily upon foliage, for not only is this likely to be consistently produced, but it is very much in sympathy with water features, especially those plants which produce grass- or rush-like foliage.

□ Grasses, rushes and reeds □

True grasses are very important plants for waterside planting. You only need to look at natural ponds and streams to see how significant a contribution the spire reed or water bamboo, *Phragmites communis*, makes. This grows in most soils and situations from standing water to dryish land. In most gardens it should be severely restricted to prevent its rapid takeover, although this exuberance can be used to advantage where a stream bank is suffering sheet erosion. Spire reed, with its bamboo-like foliage and silvery-white or purplish silky flower heads, is a first class ground stabilizer. Where greater elegance is desired, use its modest form, var. *variegatus*.

The same policy should be adopted for the giant reed, *Arundo donax*, although in Britain it is not reliably hardy. When established it is a magnificent sight, its sugar cane-like appearance lending a tropical air to the most traditional garden. In its natural habitat it can attain a height of 6 m (20 ft), but in this country it scarcely makes 2.4 m (8 ft). There is a shorter growing, more desirable kind with cream and green striped foliage, *A. donax* 'Variegata'.

□ Bamboo □

No poolside or stream garden could be considered to be complete without at least one group of hardy bamboo. For elegance, grace and tolerance of widely varying conditions, few decorative plants can compare with these handsome foliage plants. It might justifiably be said that they have no equals among hardy garden plants, for they bestow a very individual oriental charm upon a waterside, provide greenery of a light and cheerful tone, and yet only require the minimum of attention before giving of their best. There are bamboos to suit all tastes, from the tiny *Arundinaria pumila*, sporting slender waving canes barely 60 cm (2 ft) high, to the enormous cane reed, *A. gigantea*, with towering canes up to 9 m (30 ft) tall. Most gardeners prefer bamboos of medium stature, the tall species being out of place in the modern garden, while the dwarfer kinds lack the necessary height to convey the sense of grace and timelessness which is inherent in most bamboos. For today's garden few bamboos can surpass the old sinarundinarias which botanists have transferred to the arundinarias as *Arundinaria nitida* and *A. murielae*. Both are of modest proportions and neither is invasive.

Arundinaria murielae has slender yellowish canes, rarely thicker than a pencil, in clumps 1.8 m (6 ft) high, while *A. nitida* reaches a similar height, but with contrasting deep purple stems and darker pea-green leaves. *Arundinaria anceps* is another popular kind and can often be discovered in older gardens. With its tall brownish cylindrical canes and coarse pendant foliage, it is often confused with that other old favourite the common metake, *A. japonica*. But the canes of the metake are much slimmer and carry larger shiny green leaves with greyish undersides.

The majority of arundinarias enjoy partial shade, but to do really well require an ample supply of moisture. A moisture retentive soil from which surplus water can drain away freely is preferable to really swampy conditions, and so they are better suited to the streamside rather than the bog garden, especially kinds like *A. viridistriata*, *A. simonii* and the bizarre *A. quadrangularis*. Although only likely to prosper in a sheltered spot, this latter is a plantsman's delight, producing almost square stems with enlarged leaf joints and bold green pendant foliage. *Arundinaria viridistriata* is quite hardy. A majestic species with dark green canes splashed with purple which support foliage that is irregularly barred with gold and green. A strikingly handsome bamboo, this benefits from having the previous season's canes removed during the spring in order to encourage the prolific growth of colourful young foliage. The Chinese *A. simonii* is not quite so startling, but is nevertheless well worth growing. Leaf colour varies from dull to dark green, the individual leaves often being half green and half glaucous beneath. Its canes are not variable, being bold and handsome with an attractive white bloom in their juvenile state.

The canes of *Phyllostachys aurea* are a botanical peculiarity; its foliage is of more interest to the gardener. This is graceful and imparts a warm golden glow which can be used to great advantage in dreary corners. The canes themselves are rather knobbly with curiously enlarged leaf joints. The remainder of the phyllostachys all look very similar, but they are all first class garden plants. The lovely *P. viridi-glaucescens* is the most freely available. This has strong slender canes which in their early life are green, but mellow to a rich yellow and support sheaves of bright green leaves with glaucous undersides. Until fairly recently *Shibataea kumasasa* was classified as a phyllostachys. Of diminutive stature, it has curious canes of irregular and acutely angular growth which are bright green when young, but fade to dull brown with the passage of time. These produce dense clusters of broad lance-shaped leaves.

For spectacular foliage effect *Sasa tessellata* is difficult to surpass. This has glossy green leaves up to 60 cm (2 ft) long and as much as 15 cm (6 in) wide, borne on slender stems which look rather too fragile to support their weight. Despite being well known, it is not freely available other than from specialist growers. *Sasa palmata* is equally amenable, but rather vigorous and generally unsuited to the smaller garden. It is a useful plant for filling large areas where perpetual greenery and low maintenance are prime requirements.

■ *The cultivation of bamboo*

The cultivation of established bamboos presents few problems and is generally restricted to the removal of dead canes and mulching with leaf mould or well rotted manure each spring. Freshly planted bamboos are a different matter and require very careful watering for several months after transplanting if growth is to continue unchecked. Bamboos are best planted during a cool period in early summer when the young basal shoots are just in evidence. A damp friable soil in a sheltered position suits them best, although most of the commonly grown species are very tolerant and adapt to most conditions. Pot grown plants are the easiest to establish and should be knocked out of their pots and planted without disturbance. Clumps lifted from open ground lose most of their soil when lifted, but once established make more substantial plants much sooner.

A frequent problem during the initial stages of establishment is windrock, the moving of the stems and foliage by the wind which disturbs the roots and prevents them establishing quickly. Prevent by carefully reducing the height of the canes by about one third and tying the cut stems together. Untie the stems once the plants are well established.

Apart from their importance as decorative subjects, bamboos have a secondary economic value which gardeners often overlook: the production of canes for staking. Not all bamboos are suitable for this purpose, but both *Arundinaria japonica* and *A. anceps* yield suitable canes. Mature green canes should be cut during the summer and spread out to dry in a cool airy shed until the following spring when they should be ready for use.

As bamboos rarely flower or set seed, propagation is limited to division. On the occasions when bamboos do flower, the plants die afterwards, so this is not a welcome occurrence. Division of bamboos is best undertaken during the spring or early summer, the young culms or shoots from the outer part of the plant being the material to use. Never attempt to move and divide the older woody central portions of a clump. This almost always results in their loss. Young healthy culms can be potted in any good potting compost and allowed to become established. It usually takes a whole year for a proper tight rootball to develop. The bamboo is then ready for planting out.

■ *Hardy sugar cane*

Although not a true bamboo, the hardy sugar cane, *Miscanthus sacchariflorus* is closely allied; it has the same general aspect as a bamboo and it is easier to

A natural rill heavily clothed with permanent planting. The bold yellow Himalayan cowslips provide height and summer-long colour.

establish. Along with the true bamboos, miscanthus possesses a quality found in few other garden plants, that of creating magical sounds. A garden should stir all the senses and few sounds are as lovely as the whispering of bamboo foliage in a gentle breeze. Miscanthus is versatile too, happily growing in moderately damp soil at the top of a bank, but being equally at home near the water's edge.

Apart from the popular species there is a golden-leafed form called 'Aureus' and a striped foliage cultivar with green and white banded leaves known as 'Variegatus'. *Miscanthus sinensis* is grown equally as often, but by being slimmer, with narrower, somewhat hairy foliage, it does not possess the authority or dignity expressed by a plant like *M. sacchariflorus*. Nevertheless, there are many excellent garden varieties about, like the silky plumed 'Silver Feather' and banded and variegated 'Zebrinus' and 'Variegatus'. All are commendable water-side plants.

■ *Stipas*

So too are the stipas, although none will tolerate really wet soil. They are grasses for dry conditions, but with a handsome pendant habit that associates well with water. The most striking species is the bold free-flowering *Stipa calamagrostis*, but for foliage effect the elegant *S. pennata* is difficult to beat. Only the pennisetums can vie with stipas for grace and charm, but these too are grasses for free-draining places. Their habit is perfect for the waterside, particularly that of the fountain grass, *Pennisetum alopecuroides*, a plant whose common name defines an elegance which is greatly enhanced by the reflective qualities of water. Attaining a height of 90 cm (3 ft) or more, during late summer it produces frothy flowerheads amongst handsome arching foliage. A reliable perennial, it is readily divisible, although it can be raised easily from seed. The more unusual feathertop grass, *P. villosum*, is of similar habit, but diminutive stature and shorter duration. In its native East Africa it is a perennial, but in our fickle climate must be regarded as a half-hardy annual.

■ *Manna grass*

The manna grasses or glyceria are mostly perennial and truly aquatic, some of the more vulgar species having a tendency to invade. The only one that can be unreservedly recommended is the variegated leafed *Glyceria aquatica* 'Variegata'. Popularly grown as a marginal pool plant, this fast growing grass with cream and green striped foliage infused with rose-pink in the early part of the year, is most adaptable, tolerating ordinary garden conditions as well as several centimetres of water. A first class subject for eroded stream banks, but in a situation to its liking it must be vigorously controlled.

■ *Reedmaces*

The same applies to the typhas or reedmaces, those tall handsome stream and poolside plants with bold upright foliage and handsome brown poker-like heads which most people refer to as bulrushes. They are nothing of the sort, the true bulrush being the rather uninspiring green, reed-like *Scirpus lacustris*. However, most gardeners have a fondness for them, especially those who are flower arrangers too. Although very handsome, these likeable rogues should be treated with caution if they are to be introduced to the garden. For not only are they vigorous and inclined to swamp their neighbours, but they also have extremely sharp pointed, creeping rootstocks which are quite capable of puncturing any nearby liner. If kept well restrained, they are useful marginal subjects, conveying a natural waterside effect and at the same time providing much needed height. *Typha angustifolia* has narrow foliage, while that of *T. latifolia* is broad. However, while it is possible to grow these two common species successfully in the ordinary water feature, I would be more inclined to turn to *T. laxmannii* for a dependable well behaved species. With slightly smaller, but well proportioned flower spikes, this modest fellow seldom grows much more than 90 cm (3 ft) high and produces attractive willowy leaves. However, if your water feature is small and you feel that even this would be overpowering, then try the tiny Japanese *T. minima*. Rarely exceeding 45 cm (18 in) in height, this produces masses of short fat brown flower spikes amidst a waving sea of grassy foliage. Apart from its great beauty, it is well restrained and never makes itself a nuisance.

■ *Sedges*

That is not something that could be said of the sedges, especially the *Carex* species of which there are few of garden merit and many that have a tendency to become invasive if not handled carefully. The often recommended cyperus sedge, *C. pseudo-cyperus*, is one such species, a glabrous-tufted perennial with a rapidly spreading rootstock. It resembles somewhat a coarse umbrella grass – *Cyperus alternifolius* – but with sparse dark-green foliage. Curious flower spikes droop from their slender supports. The great pond sedge, *C. riparia*, is also best avoided, but a word in praise of its cultivars does not come amiss. These are restrained and lend an oriental charm to the waterside. The best known is *C. riparia* 'Bowles Golden', a much prized plant with rich golden foliage and spikes of dark brown flowers. It is temperamental until established in a situation to its liking and even then it tends to die out if subjected to persistent flooding during winter. A plant known as *C. riparia* 'Aurea' is sometimes offered by nurserymen, but I have yet to discover the differences between this and 'Bowles Golden'. *C. riparia* 'Variegata', however, is quite distinct for the leaves are attractively striped with white and green. This is an easier and far more reliable plant, which thrives in partial shade in anything up to 10 cm (4 in) of water. Do not confuse it with the very similar *C. morrowii* 'Variegata', which cannot be recommended as a permanent poolside resident in any but the mildest of areas. Few other species are worthy of consideration, with the exception of the pendulous sedge, *C. pendula*, and only then where space is not at a premium. This is a tall dignified plant, with broad green leaves and long drooping spikes of khaki catkin-like flowers, commonly encountered along shady streamsides and in damp woods.

■ *Umbrella plants*

The *Cyperus* or umbrella plants are related to the sedges. Only two species of this predominantly tropical genus are sufficiently hardy to tolerate freezing, and experts are even divided as to the hardiness of one of these, *Cyperus vegetus*. But my experience indicates that it is absolutely hardy and well worth planting in the shallow margins of large and medium-sized pools. A native of Chile, it produces tufted spikelets of reddish mahogany flowers throughout late summer from amidst spreading umbels of bright pea-green foliage. Its larger cousin the sweet galingale, *C. longus*, is a similar plant. A trifle taller with terminal umbels of stiff spiky leaves which radiate from the stem like umbrella ribs, this stout fellow is never more happy than when growing on a bank and allowed to creep down and colonize the mud at the water's edge.

■ *Bur reeds*

These conditions are also enjoyed by the bur reeds, especially the common bur reed, *Sparganium ramosum*. A rather coarse rush-like plant, it has fresh green foliage and clustered heads of brownish-green flowers that are followed by a spiky seed head that looks rather like a very small teasel. In a small water feature the bur reed is not worth considering, but for large expanses of water where ducks are to be encouraged it is of great value. This latter is one of the primary reasons for growing *Zizania*, for neither species has any outstanding visual merit, but their grain is a magnet for waterfowl. The taller and more frequently grown species is *Zizania aquatica*, a North American native with slender arching reed-like foliage up to 3 m (10 ft) high. Its Siberian cousin, *Z. latifolia*, is of more modest stature, a mere 1.2 m (4 ft) high, but is a perennial and therefore a permanent inhabitant of the waterside.

■ *Bulrushes*

So too are the true bulrushes typified by *Scirpus lacustris*, the species in which the infant Moses was said to have been cradled. This is an interesting plant for shallow water, with stiff dark-green needle-like leaves arising from short, hard, creeping rhizomes. During summer the foliage is crowned with pendant tassels of crowded reddish-brown flowers, followed by clusters of insignificant triangular fruits. A close companion, *S. tabernaemontani*, the glaucous bulrush, looks very much like a superior form of *S. lacustris* and should be grown in preference whenever possible for it has slender foliage of steely-grey with a

Careful thought must be given to planting the skunk cabbage, its huge foliage dominating the scene during the summer.

Provided the stream does not dry up completely, the associated planting will be happy. All have probing roots that spread beneath the stream bed.

conspicuous mealy bloom, and is bedecked with terminal sprays of small dark brown flowers. Although a garden-worthy plant in its own right, *S. tabernaemontani* has given rise to the outstanding zebra rush, *S.t.* 'Zebrinus', a very popular and widely commercialized mutant with stems that are alternately barred green and white. This rarely grows above 90 cm (3 ft) high, and thrives best when allowed to colonize in very shallow water. Unfortunately, plain green stems are sometimes produced and these should be removed at source, as they will rapidly outgrow the desirable variegated portion if allowed to remain. Apart from the zebra rush, the only other commonly cultivated bulrush is *S. tabernaemontani* 'Albescens', a handsome plant of uncertain origin. Its stout upright stems are a glowing sulphurous-white, conspicuously marked with thin green longitudinal stripes. These arise in clumps from thick creeping rhizomes which are frost-tender and should be protected from the vagaries of our winter climate with a layer of straw.

■ *Rushes*

The true rushes or *Juncus* species are not normally considered desirable for the water garden, for with few exceptions, they quickly become weedy and rampant, swamping their more sophisticated neighbours. However, those that are tolerable are some of the most interesting and curious aquatics a keen gardener can acquire. Two of the best and most readily obtainable are mutants of the soft rush, *Juncus effusus*, a common inhabitant of wet pastures and marshes throughout the northern hemisphere. The corkscrew rush, *Juncus effusus* 'Spiralis', is a form with curiously malformed stems that grow in a spiralling corkscrew fashion, giving the plant a strangely grotesque appearance like a Harry Lauder walking stick, while *J. effusus* 'Vittatus' is a golden variegated cultivar which grows about 60 cm (2 ft) high with alternate longitudinal stripes of green and yellow. As with many variegated plants, normal vigorous green foliage will often swamp the variegated, so destruction of any predominantly green shoots that emerge is essential.

■ *Cotton grass*

The cotton grasses are extremely useful subjects for shallow margins, particularly where there is a tendency towards acidity. They are absolutely hardy but unfortunately few of the many species seem to be in general cultivation. *Eriophorum angustifolium* is the one commonly commercialized and undoubtedly the most useful. With its evergreen grassy foliage and cotton wool-like seeding heads, it makes a welcome contribution to the poolside during early summer. A similar, but larger species, the broad-leafed cotton grass, *E. latifolium*, is sometimes grown but seems to be very short-lived under cultivation. However, anyone who can successfully establish a clump will be well rewarded with a memorable display of dainty pendant spikelets of cotton wool, which if picked in their full glory, dry admirably for floral decoration.

□ Foliage and form □

As I intimated at the outset, the streamside planter has to depend heavily upon foliage, not just to give solidity to the planting, but to provide some kind of form and structure that is not fleeting. Of all the moisture-loving foliage plants, the most permanent and structural are the phormiums. Natives of New Zealand they are popularly known as New Zealand flax because of the strong leaf fibres which they produce that for centuries have been used in the manufacture of rope and twine.

■ *Phormiums*

There are two species. The true New Zealand flax, *Phormium tenax*, which has enormous iris-like leaves up to 1.8 m (6 ft) high and the mountain flax, *P. cookianum*, which is of more modest stature and rarely grows more than 1.2 m (4 ft) tall. Both species enjoy moist, but not waterlogged conditions and between them have sired many colourful cultivars. All have startling foliage, which in 'Cream Delight' is vivid creamy-yellow banded with green. 'Dark Delight' provides a perfect contrast with its deep maroon leaves and 'Emerald Green' is a much smaller kind with bright green foliage. 'Tricolor' is loved by some, but others find it bizarre, its multi-coloured leaves splashed and banded with white, rose and green. The taller kinds are dominated by the striking bronze and carmine banded 'Dazzler' and a race of fascinating modern kinds with the prefix Maori. 'Maori Maiden' is the shortest one with boldly banded leaves of red, pink and brown, but the taller 'Maori Chief' and 'Maori Sunrise' also command attention.

The diversity of colour offered by modern phormiums gives the gardener ample opportunities for experimenting with complementary and contrasting colour schemes. On the other hand phormiums can be used to great effect as individuals, the nicest way to show them off being in damp soil right at the pool or streamside where their glory can be reflected all about them. Although not lime-lovers, phormiums perform tolerably well on alkaline soil providing that there is sufficient moisture available. In any event it is desirable to incorporate liberal quantities of coarse peat or well rotted compost into the soil as they respond to generous amounts of organic matter. Although evergreen, leaves are constantly being replaced and by the end of the summer there will be many untidy ones. While it is permissible to trim off dead and decaying material, it is wise to leave as much foliage as possible to protect the crowns through the winter.

■ *Gunneras*

Some measure of protection is also desirable for *Gunnera manicata*, particularly in colder areas. A covering of straw or bracken, or with established plants, their own frost blackened leaves, is usually sufficient to prevent damage to the over-wintering buds. This is one of the largest and certainly most remarkable herbaceous plants that can be grown outside. Although to the uninitiated it has the appearance of a giant rhubarb, closer inspection will reveal several differences. Its leaves are large, up to 1.8 m (6 ft) across, and more or less kidney-shaped. The margins are deeply indented and the undersides and leaf stalks are liberally sprinkled with unpleasant bristly hairs. The much branching flower spike is not exotic or spectacular, but curious, like a huge red-green bottle brush that may be anything between 30–90 cm (1–3 ft) high. It arises from a thick creeping rhizome that is densely clothed in brown papery scales, which during the winter months have been likened to a reclining bear. Gunneras like a moist cool position in which to grow, the ideal situation from both an aesthetic and cultural point of view being alongside a stream where their huge spreading leaves can be mirrored in rippling water, a position where moisture is plentiful but stagnation avoided. Apart from *G. manicata*, there are several other rarer species including the similar, slightly smaller, *G. chilensis*. Other than in size, and shape of rhizome and leaf, of which the latter is not particularly apparent, there is little to commend it in preference to the more readily available *G. manicata*.

■ *Decorative rhubarbs*

Of course not every garden can accommodate this majestic plant, but in a confined space some of the decorative rhubarbs, with their broad spreading leaves and handsome flower spikes can attempt to emulate it. *Rheum palmatum* is the most widely grown species with broad spreading foliage and spikes of creamy-white blooms some 1.5–1.8 m (5–6 ft) high. A variety called *tanguticum* has much divided foliage and crimson or deep rose flowers, while the cultivar 'Bowles Crimson' or 'Atropurpureum' as it is sometimes known, has foliage suffused with deep purplish-red. Several other species are cultivated, but only *R. nobile*, a curious variety with 1.2 m (4 ft) high spires of fawn coloured bracts, is at home in the bog garden. The others are much happier in the wild garden or shrubbery.

■ *Hostas*

The manicured garden is certainly the place for those most attractive of decorative foliage plants, the funkias or hostas. It is generally conceded that the variegated forms are the most desirable, the tongue twisting *Hosta undulata medio-variegata* being the most colourful, with slightly contorted foliage in a mixture of cream, white and green, while the larger hybrid 'Thomas Hogg' has more orderly leaves of bright green, boldly edged with white. *Hosta glauca marginata* also has variegated margins to its leaves and is a variety of one of the best plain foliage species, *H. glauca*. *Hosta plantaginea*, with its big heart-shaped leaves and slightly fragrant white trumpet-shaped blossoms borne during summer, is the aristocrat of the family, better even than the popular *H. fortunei* and its forms. *Hosta lancifolia* is smaller than the others and has long stalked racemes of lavender-blue flowers above compact tufts of rich green leaves. A number of different forms of this are grown, but none are finer than the golden-green foliage variety 'Aurea' and the very large 'Fortis'. Unfortunately the naming of hostas is in a terrible muddle and therefore any greater discussion upon the diversity within this plant group here would be folly, for we would not necessarily be evaluating the same plant. If you are going to grow hostas, then get out to your local nursery and choose by visual appeal rather than name.

■ *Houttuynia cordata*

There is no confusion over *Houttuynia cordata*, for this most amenable little fellow is on its own in a single genus. It has handsome bluish–green heart-shaped leaves and small white four-petalled flowers with hard central cones, although in the double flowered form 'Plena' these are lost in a dense central ruff of petals. Apart from these there is a bizarre multi-coloured foliage form which I find displeasing, for it looks virus-ridden and sickly. Known variously as 'Variegata' and 'Tricolor', it is appreciated by some. All three should be allowed to creep about at will and carpet the ground beneath taller growing rushes, although they can equally well stand alone as bold foliage subjects at the water's edge.

■ *Arrowheads*

The arrowheads are waterside plants of a happy disposition, growing equally well in mud or right in the water. They spread quite quickly by means of runners, which at the approach of winter develop large ovoid turions or winter buds at their extremities. These look like iris bulbs and are popularly known as duck potatoes as wild ducks will forage about in the mud and dig them up during the winter months if given the opportunity. *Sagittaria sagittifolia* and *S. japonica* are the most popular species. The white flowers of *S. sagittifolia* having black and crimson centres, while those of *S. japonica* are yellow. There is also a very fine double form of the latter called 'Flore Pleno', with flowers like tiny white powder puffs. All the popular kinds have ribbon-like submerged foliage and long stemmed arrow-like aerial leaves which in deep water will often float. All arise from leafy sheaths at the base of the plant, together with the flower spike which bears the tiered whorls of tri-petalled blooms. Apart from the common kinds, the only other species encountered in cultivation is *S. latifolia*. Under favourable conditions in slightly acid mud, this splendid plant is capable of attaining a height of 1.2–1.5 m (4–5 ft), with handsome soft green awl-shaped leaves and sprays of snow-white flowers. Many different forms have been described, but those most likely to be found are *S. latifolia* var. *pubescens*, with hairy foliage, and *S. latifolia* 'Flore Pleno' with double flowers.

■ *Sweet flag*

The sweet flag, *Acorus calamus*, prospers under similar conditions. A member of the arum family, this is often mistaken for an iris on account of its flat linear leaves and flat fleshy rhizomes. The ordinary species has shiny fresh green foliage and curious greenish-yellow horn-like flower spikes. The leaves are

Ferns are versatile plants for difficult damp spots, filling awkward pockets in this rocky watercourse. Native species are especially adaptable.

fragrant and in years gone by were used for strewing, so that when trodden on an aroma of tangerines would be wafted upon the air. A plant of architectural merit, it is more often cultivated in its cream and green variegated form, *A.c.* 'Variegatus', not just for its striking summer foliage, but that of early spring which is strongly suffused with red. Of all the variegated streamside plants this is one of the loveliest and most resilient.

■ *Water plantains*
Persistence is also a quality for which the water plantains are noted, but this is not always appreciated for they have a tendency to seed quite freely and in a natural setting can become quite a nuisance. However, there are two very interesting species that can be relied upon to behave themselves reasonably well. Of these the most familiar is *Alisma plantago-aquatica*, a handsome plant with attractive ovate foliage and loose pyramidal panicles of pink and white flowers. The broad towering spires become hard and woody after flowering and persist throughout the winter, catching the snow on their outspread arms, in a most attractive manner. *Alisma parviflora* is of similar habit, but with distinct rounded leaves that during autumn and winter fall into the water and become completely and most beautifully skeletonized. Its pyramids of pink and white flowers are shorter than those of its cousin and render it more suitable for the smaller water feature.

■ *Water docks*
Few gardeners would consider introducing dock to their gardens, but the water dock, *Rumex hydrolapathum* is an exception. Attaining a height of 1.8–2.4 m (6–8 ft) under favourable conditions, it is well suited to the larger water feature. It looks rather like an enlarged version of the common garden dock, but with bold dark green foliage which changes colour through bronze to crimson at the approach of autumn. A variety from Manchuria called *R. hydrolapathum* var. *maximus* is even more lovely, with larger leaves, although the plant is of smaller stature. Like the water plantains, the water docks spread rather freely from seed, so the removal of old flower heads is advisable if you wish to control their distribution.

■ *Water willow*
The water willow, *Decodon verticillatus*, is usually regarded in a similar light, for this too is a rather coarse and vulgar plant, but one which should be considered for its outstanding autumn colour. Pinkish at the approach of autumn, by the time the first hard frosts of winter defoliate it, the leaves have passed through rose and vermilion to an intense fiery crimson. A native of North America it has tall willowy stems and sprays of rose-pink tubular flowers.

■ *Arrow arums*
Another group of streamside plants from the New World are the arrow arums or peltandras. *Peltandra virginica* is the common sort. A handsome plant with narrow green spathes, and bold, dark green, glossy arrow-shaped foliage. *Peltandra alba* is more modest, but with large greenish or white spathes of little significance. Of all the hardy relatives of the arum the peltandras have the finest foliage, boldly sculptured leaves that provide a startling feature at the water's edge when used alone. Not as individual plants, but a bold group, arrows pointing skyward like a well ordered army marching into the water.

□ Poolside favourites □

While many of the plants already under consideration grow happily in a little water or merely mud, and are consequently poolside favourites too, there is a clearly defined group which are not used with such flexibility. These are the ones that disguise the harsh pool or streamside edge, particularly where the water feature has been artificially contrived, or the use of artificial materials has been necessary to correct an erosion problem. They can be used elsewhere of course, but because of their creeping or billowing habit we tend to restrict their planting to such situations. These then are what I consider to be poolside favourites.

The bog arum, *Calla palustris* is a splendid plant for masking the edge of the pool, spreading in all directions by means of stout creeping rhizomes clothed in handsome glossy heart-shaped leaves. Its flowers belie the plant's close affinity to the florist's arum, being smaller, but otherwise almost identical, and borne like tiny white sails in a sea of dark-green foliage. They are succeeded by spikes of succulent red berries filled with viable seed which, if sown immediately it ripens, forms a quick and inexpensive means of propagating this valuable plant.

■ *Water forget-me-nots*

Seed raising is the most usual means of propagating the water forget-me-not too, although the division of emerging young crowns early in the spring is normally successful. The former method has the added advantage that a plant or two of the white form may be raised. Although not quite as robust, it makes an unusual and extremely attractive addition when planted amongst the azure hummocks of its conventional neighbours. Not that people are as familiar with the water forget-me-not, *Myosotis scorpioides*, as they should be. During early summer this charming little fellow is absolutely smothered in sky blue flowers that resemble almost exactly those of its bedding plant cousin. An improved variety known as 'Semperflorens' is superior to the common kinds, producing fewer leaves and being less inclined to straggle across the mud. Some years ago a cultivar called 'Mermaid' was introduced and is often still listed, but as far as I can tell is no different from the typical species. All water forget-me-nots are lovely though and can be thoroughly recommended as plants for camouflaging as well as floral display.

■ *Bugles*

The same can be said for the bugles or ajugas. These are invaluable for their colourful display as well as their ability to hide a harsh edge. The common *Ajuga reptans* can be a bit of a nuisance, but its varieties 'Purpurea' with purplish-bronze leaves and the pinkish-buff and cream variegated 'Multicolor' are not at all invasive and carpet the ground with foliage of excellent substance. *Ajuga pyramidalis* has plain green leaves, but is outstanding for its substantial spikes of gentian blue flowers which pale the drab navy blue ones of the others into insignificance. *Ajuga genevensis* is often recommended for poolside planting, but it is not a plant for the bog garden, rather it is a plant to allow to spread from the drier reaches of the ordinary garden up to the water's edge. Unlike its comrades it does not grow from runners, but just spreads outwards in the course of living. Its flowers are blue or occasionally white or pink and borne in spikes during early summer.

□ Other favourites □

The strongly aromatic water mint, *Mentha aquatica*, enjoys shallow water or wet mud and when growing happily produces, throughout late summer, dense terminal whorls of lilac pink flowers on slender reddish stems amidst an abundance of hairy greyish-green foliage. Unfortunately, it is inclined to spread rather rapidly by means of its slender rhizomes and therefore cannot be recommended for the smaller garden. The common lizard's tail, *Saururus cernuus*, certainly can. This is a rather bizarre, but nevertheless attractive aquatic plant for shallow water. It produces clumps of heart-shaped foliage, which often assume bronze autumnal tints, and quaint nodding terminal sprays of creamy-white flowers during summer. A rarer species called *S. loureiri* is sometimes grown and this has paler foliage and erect rather than nodding sprays of flowers.

There are a great number of species of lysimachia around, but the most useful to the waterside gardener is creeping Jenny, *L. nummularia*, and its golden-leafed form 'Aurea'. This is a more or less evergreen carpeting plant that is ideal for masking the edge of a pool or providing an attractive ground cover between taller growing marsh plants in the bog garden. It seldom exceeds 5 cm (2 in) in height and is studded with starry buttercup-like blooms during summer. The marsh hypericum, *Hypericum elodes*, is also a useful plant especially for shallow water or wet mud. Forming a dense carpet of foliage it hides the often ugly point where pool structure meets land and gives an added

Opposite: *Subtle hues and contrasting textures of foliage demonstrate that brilliant colour is not essential to make a pleasing picture.*
Below: *The variegated water grass is marching out into the pool. Natural plantings like this need to be reduced regularly.*

bonus of showy yellow flowers during late summer. *Preslia cervina* is of similar disposition, a plant which in recent years has seen a jump in popularity. It forms spreading clumps, with slender erect stems densely clothed in small lanceolate leaves, and is crowned during late summer with stiff whorled spikes of dainty ultramarine or lilac flowers. The whole plant is strongly aromatic and is happiest when growing in very shallow water.

So is the only truly aquatic veronica, the ever popular brooklime, *Veronica beccabunga*. Like many of its terrestrial cousins it has dark blue flowers with a white eye. But here the similarity ends, for these are not borne in familiar terminal spikes but in the axils of the leaves of trailing procumbent stems. Veronica, although not a spectacular plant, has many uses and is invaluable for climbing out of the water and masking the area where pool meets land. It will also spread across the surface of the water, providing shade for the fish, and its hanging roots are a suitable place for the deposition of spawn. The common mare's tail, *Hippuris vulgaris*, is no great beauty either. It is a plant often despised, particularly in places where it grows locally abundantly and makes itself a nuisance. For this reason it is seldom recommended for the water garden, but in a shady or fast-moving stream it is ideal, thriving in adversity and thrusting up simple spikes of narrow whorled leaves. The perfect plant in fast-flowing streams for marrying the land with the water. For features with still water, this role could be better filled by a charming fellow known as brass buttons, *Cotula coronopifolia*. Although the majority of this large family of daisy-like plants are popularly grown in the rock garden, this one species is truly aquatic and, being dwarf, of immense value around the edges of smaller water features. Its bright golden flowers are like a smaller version of those of a dandelion and borne in profusion above strongly scented light green foliage. Unfortunately it is a monocarpic species, dying as soon as flowering is over, but if left undisturbed usually seeds itself and is then in all but name a perennial.

□ Plants for dry conditions □

At the moment we have only considered those plants which will grow at the poolside in very damp or wet conditions. Of course, in reality the poolside fringe is often quite dry and yet the pool still needs tying to the surrounding garden. This applies equally when a bog garden is contrived independently in its own right or as a separate entity alongside a pool. Such constructions often leave ribbons and patches of open ground which need clothing with aesthetically appropriate plants.

■ *Dutch iris*
Surprisingly one of the most suitable groups of plants are the bulbous Dutch iris. The delight of the florist, but also the pool and streamside gardener. Forget that they are bulbous for a moment, and visualize their marvellous upright sword-like leaves and handsome brightly coloured flowers reflected in the water. Where you are unable to accommodate true aquatic or bog irises, these are a first class substitute.

Treat them very much like daffodils or tulips, planting the bulbs in the autumn in an open sunny position. They have few demands during their growing season and if allowed to die down naturally after flowering will become permanently established. There are many lovely cultivars to choose from, but the light blue flowered 'Wedgwood' is among the loveliest.

■ *Fuchsias*

Fuchsias are not often associated with water features. However, they are among the loveliest plants for damp, but not waterlogged ground at the pool or streamside, their colourful tear-like pendant blossoms reflecting beautifully in clear water. Usually thought of as an indoor plant, hybridizers have been busily working to improve the hardy kinds, so that now there are almost as many good readily available varieties of hardy fuchsias as there are tender kinds.

Of course the winter can present a problem, for even hardy varieties will not tolerate severe weather if not properly established. So early planting is vital if the plants are to become a lasting feature of the waterside. It is best to begin with substantial plants growing in large pots during early summer. As the plants have probably been established from cuttings taken during the previous summer, they will have spent all their life under glass. While strong early growth is to be recommended, it is important that they are properly hardened off, so prior to planting they should be exposed to life in a cold frame for two or three weeks. Plant firmly, ensuring that each rootball is slightly beneath the previous soil line.

Summer cultivation should ensure that the plants do not dry out, especially in the early stages of their establishment. Each spring it is useful to mulch around the plants with a generous layer of peat or well rotted garden compost in order to conserve moisture. If newly established plants do not break readily and form a shapely bush, they should be encouraged to do so by regularly pinching out.

There are innumerable cultivars to choose from, but the lovely single 'Corallina' with scarlet and purple blossoms, together with the semi-double scarlet and violet-purple 'Drame' have the kind of habit that is most appropriate at the water's edge. The bold, upright 'Chillerton Beauty' with its myriad single mauve and pink blossoms is another first class kind, especially if associated with lower growing varieties like the golden leafed 'Genii'.

■ *Convolvulus*

Most gardeners would hold up their hands in horror at growing bindweeds at the waterside, but those who investigate a little further may be surprised to learn that apart from the pernicious species which invade our gardens, there are a number of well mannered kinds of exceptional beauty which enjoy scrambling around in the full sun in just the kind of conditions that are regularly found at the artificial pool or streamside.

Probably the best known is the annual *Convolvulus tricolor*. This is a sprawling plant with hairy foliage sprinkled with saucer-shaped blooms of blue and maroon shading through white to pale sulphurous yellow at the throat. Several named varieties have been raised with distinctive blossoms of consistent colouring, but none possesses the charm of the species or its more tidy form var. *compactus*. An early spring sowing where they are to flower will ensure a continuous display of colour from early summer until the first autumn frost. *Convolvulus pentapetaloides* requires similar treatment, erupting in a mass of brilliant blue flowers amidst handsome prostrate foliage and providing colour for a similar period. For covering a sunny bank at pool or streamside few plants can compare, except of course for its cousin *C. aureus superbus*, a more vigorous kind with dark green heart-shaped leaves and rich golden yellow blossoms. Although technically a perennial, this amenable fellow will flower profusely from an early sowing the same year.

■ Kirengeshoma

Amongst the more unusual plants for the waterside is *Kirengeshoma palmata*, a strange herbaceous member of the hydrangea family. A native of Japan, this handsome fellow produces large leaves which are divided like a maple. On contented plants growing in a moist situation these may be as much as 30 cm (1 ft) across and carried proudly on slender cane-like stems a metre or so high. Soft yellow flowers are produced during late summer in lax terminal clusters. These are bell-shaped, waxy, and would be of considerable merit if only they would open fully and expose their beauty. Instead they cluster together hiding their faces like a group of silly giggling school girls. However, kirengeshoma is worth growing for its foliage alone.

■ Acanthus

The various acanthus are more bold, one could even say regal, unashamedly thrusting up dense rigid spikes of white, purple or rose flowers. But it is their foliage that I love, those gorgeous glossy, evergreen, much divided leaves, which in *Acanthus mollis* are often 60 cm (2 ft) long. The best acanthus for foliage effect is the pinkish-white flowered *A. mollis* var. *latifolius*, although the somewhat shorter dull purple *A. spinosus*, with more finely divided and prickly leaves, has much to commend it. Both are easily raised from seed sown during spring or root cuttings taken in the autumn and are first class focal plants.

■ Meadow rues

While acanthus are stately and better grown as specimen plants uncluttered by tall and fussy neighbours, the thalictrums or meadow rues are definitely background subjects. With their delicate lacy maidenhair-like foliage they provide a perfect foil for brightly coloured marsh plants. There are many species, but only *Thalictrum dipterocarpum* is widely cultivated. A tall growing plant, in excess of 1.2 m (4 ft), it has billowing masses of finely divided green leaves with a dull purplish cast, and bears a profusion of tiny purple blossoms with conspicuous yellow anthers, which in 'Hewitt's Double' are even more showy. A lesser known species, *T. speciosissimum* is even more lovely. Known variously as *T. flavum* subsp. *glaucum* and just plain *T. glaucum*, this produces compact hummocks of steely-blue foliage scarcely more than a metre high. I prize this little gem not only for its foliage, but its contrasting mass of fluffy sulphurous blossoms which crown the plant like froth on a Guinness. It is easily raised from seed and unlike *T. dipterocarpum* can be divided.

■ Lady's mantle

Lady's mantle, *Alchemilla mollis*, is an excellent plant to associate with meadow rues, for its rounded leaves are not only of contrasting shape, but a pleasant shade of light green that blends well with the purplish and metallic hues of the thalictrums. The loose panicles of yellowish flowers are rather dull, but the soft silky hairs which clothe both stems and leaves give the plant an attractive silvery sheen. This appearance is further enhanced after a shower of rain, as these soft hairs support glistening droplets of water which in a gentle breeze chase about the leaves like quicksilver.

The orange daylilies are popular for herbaceous borders but, like many other common perennials, flourish at the water's edge.

CHAPTER FIVE

THE PEAT GARDEN

Many gardeners believe that a peat garden is rather like a rock garden, a place where those plants from mountainous regions which demand a damp organic medium are grown. It is true that many of the skills of the alpine gardener are necessary for the successful management of a peat garden, but the feature itself is more akin in environmental terms to the bog garden than the rock garden.

□ Choosing a site □

Unlike most other features a peat garden benefits from a partially shaded position, and preferably one that faces north. A densely shaded situation is not suitable as few of the plants popularly grown in peat gardens respond to such conditions. Almost all come from a cool environment with dappled shade. Often plants like dwarf rhododendrons grow naturally in an acid organic medium beneath trees with a high leaf canopy and it is this kind of environment that we should seek to create. Cool, damp conditions are not only necessary for the plants, but the peat blocks as well. If exposed to bright sun they dry up and shrink, causing the block walls to collapse and disturbing the plants. Once dried out, it is extremely difficult to wet them again and for their original shape to return.

The soil conditions of the potential site for a peat feature must also be carefully assessed, for although dampness is desired, a certain amount of drainage is necessary. As a peat garden is almost always an artificial construction on top of the existing ground, rather than a feature which 'grows' out of it, the base needs to be broken up at the very least. Compacted soil should be forked over and if the soil is heavy, then it is essential to provide some drainage, so that the peat garden does not become sodden and inhospitable to the plants.

Many gardeners will be faced with a flat site for the construction of their peat garden. For most other features this is desirable, but for a peat garden a sloping site is to be preferred. It is always visually more appealing if the block construction appears to emerge naturally from the landscape rather than being placed on it. Where a site is flat and exposed, it is desirable to create a slope or mound so that a north facing aspect can be created to suit those special plants that demand cool shade, and contours can be given to the feature to add interest.

□ Building a peat garden □

Before starting your peat garden it is advisable to understand a little of the principles involved and the nature of the materials which you are going to use. Unlike a rock garden where the rocks are a permanent visible feature, the peat garden is constructed so that ultimately its structure is completely clothed with plants. Peat blocks are not rock substitutes, they are a means of developing a specific kind of environment and terrain, and are themselves a constituent part of the growing medium. Without a healthy covering of plants, peat blocks have a very short life. They are quite unnatural, being cut out of peat turf in squares or oblongs and treated by the gardener rather like building bricks.

■ Types of peat

There are many different kinds of peat, a natural medium which has been formed by the accumulation of partially decomposed vegetation submerged in very acid water for a long period of time. Peat is variable and careful inspection should be made of the material you are going to use from the outset. From the gardener's point of view peat is divided into two main groups: the moss peats and the sedge peats. The moss peats are coarse, very fibrous and the best for the production of good quality peat blocks. The sedge peats are the very fine black or dark brown crumbly peats used in soilless composts. Even in their unrefined state they are totally unsuitable for block production. When purchased from the nursery or garden centre they are usually refined and perfect for mixing with soil into the growing medium. Ideally peat blocks should be of moss peat and cut from the upper layer of the turf. Blocks cut from lower down in the profile seem to be very acid and unhealthy looking, often developing an unsightly whitish deposit when exposed to the air.

Blocks are available in a range of sizes according to the whim of the cutter. Tiny blocks are not desirable, but those about the size of an ordinary house brick or a little larger are perfect. Nowadays these are often prepacked in small numbers for retail sales in polythene sacks. This is a convenient method of purchasing them, but be sure that they have not been lying around with the retailer for a long time and become hard and dry. Such blocks are not worth purchasing. Ideally blocks should be cut from the moor and delivered to your door still laden with natural moisture!

■ Preparation of peat blocks

If when you get your peat blocks home they are moist, but not wet, soak them in a tub of water. Although they become very heavy when laden with water they will be perfect for construction work. No two peat blocks are alike, and some that have become dried, may well have curled. Once the blocks are thoroughly soaked they will be their final shapes and dimensions and can be pared with a sharp knife if they are of uneven symmetry. At least the base, top surface and face of each should be reasonably smooth and flat.

Most peat gardens are built on a terraced principle, succeeding layers of low walls containing a friable peaty growing medium. Few gardeners wish to take these terraces more than three blocks high, for unless there is a substantial background of banking or something similar, they not only look out of place, but are difficult to get at to maintain properly. In their early stages free-standing peat gardens are not very stable; it is only when the plants' roots knit the blocks together that they become more rigid.

Above: *One of the delights of waterside planting is the opportunity of being able to create reflective pictures in the cool glassy stillness of the water.*
Opposite: *Oriental bamboos dripping with bright green foliage lend a tropical air to this waterside. Bold hostas provide a striking contrast.*

■ Starting to build

Blocks of peat are laid in the same manner as bricks, the joints of alternate layers lying at the centre of the block above and beneath (Fig. 5). Ideally the blocks should fit tightly together, but this is often impossible. Where the equivalent of a mortar joint is required, then mix a little peat with some heavy soil and make a peat/soil 'mortar'. Peat and soil should be used in about equal parts by volume. This enables the irregularities between blocks to be coped with. Some gardeners use peat alone for this purpose, but if a dry spell comes along it quickly shrinks and falls out, so while it is the perfectionist's way of doing things, it is not the most practical. Not that the soil and peat alternative should be allowed to dry out either, for this will crack and fall away in segments if not regularly moistened until the plants take hold.

The first row of blocks should be arranged on a prepared level or evenly sloping base, a generous layer of peat/soil 'mortar' having been laid. Although seemingly perverse, it is useful to be able to level the blocks with the aid of a narrow board and spirit level. Absolute evenness is not desired, but a general levelness is very necessary if the peat garden is to look right. Not only must each block be tolerably level with its neighbour, but it should also slope back slightly. This is vital for the higher layers which otherwise have a tendency to dislodge and tumble out, especially after frosty weather.

As the terrace walls are being built, a good peaty soil mixture should be prepared for back filling. There is no particular formula for this, but it should be at least half peat and half soil by volume. Your local soil is alright unless it is extremely light or else alkaline. Almost all peat garden plants will not tolerate limy soil, so if the pH of your soil is 7 or above it would be prudent to buy soil in. Remember also that by adding 50% inert peat to the growing medium you are also diluting its nutrient value, therefore a sprinkling of a general balanced fertilizer should be mixed in. Most peat-loving plants are not gross feeders, but a balanced nutrient diet is vital.

If a large area is being planted the extensive use of peat may seem to be rather expensive. To some extent this can be overcome by only providing a good, friable peaty soil where plant roots will penetrate. Therefore, if your terracing takes you 60 cm (2 ft) high, there is no need to have 60 cm (2 ft) of prepared medium when the plants' roots are only going to penetrate 30 cm (1 ft). The lower 30 cm (1 ft) can be ordinary garden soil or even brick rubble. Remember that plants will also be growing in the walls and therefore the medium immediately behind the blocks must be of good quality, for roots will penetrate at least 30 cm (1 ft).

■ Possible problems

Peat garden construction is not too difficult if the foregoing considerations are made. However, there are elements outside your control that sometimes cause problems. Birds are the most common of these, especially blackbirds, which delight in scratching and tearing the blocks apart. Voles and mice also delight in inhabiting the walls, and so some precautions should be taken. I would not suggest these where there is no evidence of vermin damage, but where trouble is brewing it can be minimized by netting the blocks with small, black plastic fruit cage netting. If stretched tightly over the walls this is not too unsightly and does offer a great measure of protection. Peg the netting into the blocks with metal meat skewers. Small holes can be cut where plants are inserted and these will eventually take over the role of the netting, hiding it completely from view.

Fig. 5 *Construction of peat garden.*

(b) Blocks should be laid back at an angle to aid stability.

(a) Build blocks in the same manner as bricks in a wall, tying joints alternately. Use curved contours rather than acute ones.

(c) The peat-walled feature is filled with a very peaty soil mix.

(d) Pot-grown, peat-loving plants can be planted in the soil mix as well as in crevices between peat blocks.

□ Getting in the plants □

A peat garden is ideally constructed during the autumn and early winter so that it can settle down before planting. Inevitably, there will be areas that need topping up with additional compost and also blocks that need realigning, so it is sensible to resist the temptation of planting immediately after construction. The plants also establish more rapidly if planted in early spring rather than the autumn. The only exception are spring and early summer flowering bulbs. Where these are to be planted in a newly established feature it is better to get them established in pots during the winter and remove them with potball intact in early spring.

Opposite: *Cool, clear, dark water glints amongst the heavily planted edges of this gentle rill. The bold foliage of rheum dominates the scene.*
Below: *A solidly planted waterside, visually appealing both from the bank above and across the water.*

There is a wide diversity of plants suitable for peat garden culture, but most are sold in pots. Only a few of the more shrubby plants are likely to be dug from open ground and then these are likely to have a decent rootball. Providing they can be kept moist, all will establish readily in the spring. Often pot grown plants are spotted in a nursery during late spring or early summer in full leaf and flower. A great temptation, but one that can only be accommodated if care is taken. If you plant out pot grown subjects during the summer do not disturb the rootball. Also watch the watering carefully. Very leafy plants may also benefit from a little additional shading until properly established.

The majority of plants will be planted into the compost mixture rather than into the walls of the peat garden. As I have already indicated most will be pot grown and if planted in the spring will just be bursting into life. It is inevitable with pot grown plants, particularly those that have overwintered as such, that they will have fairly congested root systems. Where they are pot bound do not merely knock them out of the pot and drop them in a hole in the medium, but help the roots to break out more quickly by splitting the ball open. This involves the use of a sharp knife to cut the rootball open in two or three places to permit roots to escape quickly into fresh soil.

This is absolutely essential for woody plants. If not released from their congestion, they will just sit in the soil, develop very little root and after two or three years it may still be possible to hold the plant by the top and just lift it out of the soil. A few root hairs may have been produced, but the major roots will still be twisted and contorted in their original configuration. The plant will have been existing merely on the moisture and nutrients that have been absorbed by the existing rootball. Of course, wherever possible it is preferable to plant pot grown subjects that have just reached the point where they require repotting.

Most plants will be planted merely by excavating a hole with a trowel the size of the pot ball, the plant being dropped into the hole and gently firmed in, care being taken to see that the soil level is the same as that at the surface of the pot. Only if a few roots are exposed is it permissible to plant slightly deeper. Those plants destined for the wall have to be removed from their pots and the majority of soil shaken from their roots. They are then planted between the blocks. Never attempt to plant into a block, even if you make an excavation and fill it with a suitable medium. It does not work satisfactorily. Plants planted in the peat/soil 'mortar' between blocks establish readily and quite naturally colonize the blocks in due course. It is vital to know your plants though, for a number of peat lovers resent disturbance, and although they may be potential colonizers, if they resent root disturbance they cannot be interfered with. Ideal wall plants are those that can be planted bare-rooted and also have the ability to form a spreading carpet.

■ Special conditions

A few plants will benefit from special conditions. Maybe some extra peat, the addition of grit or a richer medium. Although a peat garden is not as conveniently compartmentalized as a rock garden with its physically isolated pockets, special conditions can be created and the plants largely isolated from the surrounding medium. Sinking containers or pots in the soil is not often satisfactory, even though it may seem so in theory. Moisture content is so difficult to assess in mediums contained in plunged plastic pots and pans, the plants often becoming waterlogged. A far better container is the aquatic planting basket. This is a plastic lattice work container which will retain the soil, but will not totally restrict the roots and will ensure that the compost within is of the same dampness. A further advantage of this method of isolation is that the plant can be lifted periodically and divided without disturbing the rest of the peat garden. Just dig up the container and the entire plant comes out cleanly with it.

□ Arranging plants in the peat garden □

The arrangement of plants in the peat garden is a personal fancy. It depends whether you are an artistic gardener or a plant fanatic. Most peat gardens seem to have been built by the latter, an enthusiast who loves plants for themselves rather than the contribution that they can make to the overall garden scene. While one can sympathise with this attitude, for a peat garden creates some very special places and conditions, nevertheless it can be a truly visual experience too with the careful placement of plants in bold groups. Do not be a spotty or patchy planter. Aim to cover most of the soil surface and attempt to do it with groups of three or five plants, except perhaps when dealing with woody subjects. A permanent thread of small shrubs, preferably evergreen should run through the peat garden to give it a permanent structure, especially during winter. This helps to tie the feature to the surrounding garden if cleverly executed. Like a rock garden, peat terraces can look completely contrived and isolated unless tasteful planting ties it to its surroundings. Such planting needs to be in evidence the whole year through, so shrubs like dwarf rhododendrons, pernettya and fothergilla are invaluable in providing a degree of permanence.

As with herbaceous plants in a border, groups of odd numbers are desirable. The peat garden can be arranged in a similar fashion to an herbaceous or mixed border with the plants grading down from the tallest at the back to the shortest towards the front. I prefer a more informal approach, but I do feel that it is important to plant with a view to covering both the soil and walls with foliage. When making your design, bear in mind the maintenance aspect. The gardener does not have a long reach and needs to get in amongst the plants regularly for maintenance. By its very nature the medium will be soft and spongy and unable to accommodate even a modest foot without consequence, so it is useful in a feature like this to discreetly incorporate a few stepping stones. They need only be small pieces of paving sunk into the medium to soil level. As long as they can take a decent-sized foot, they will be large enough and an invaluable asset when you undertake regular maintenance.

■ Microclimates

Bear in mind when planting, the opportunity of creating microclimates. Even the most modest structure can have its conditions altered by the strategic placing of shrubs and plants. Aesthetics are important, but the effect of a plant upon its neighbour must be carefully considered, particularly if that effect is the cause of a nuisance as is often the case when plants like crepis and cymbalaria become established and scatter seed asunder. Beneficial effects, such as shelter must always be considered as well as the close association of plants with identical soil requirements. Careful thought should be put into every aspect of the peat garden from the planning to the execution. Once planted it becomes an addictive form of gardening, but one which is easy to practise once the conditions have been properly provided.

CHAPTER SIX

PEAT-LOVING PLANTS

The number of plants that enjoy life in a peaty growing medium is legion. One only has to consider how well many plants grow in a soilless compost to realize the opportunities offered by a peat garden. However, the potential number of suitable candidates is reduced somewhat by the character of such a feature, for it is usually contrived so that at least part of it is shaded, and acid dampness is dominant. So the environment sets limits upon what will grow successfully and become one of our peat-loving plants.

□ Background plants □

All garden features demand a suitable background and appropriate planting to link them visually with their surroundings. In most cases woody plants are the most suitable. Care must be taken with a peat garden that the shrubby planting does not visually dominate the scene and therefore dwarf varieties should be used. These must be carefully selected though, for dwarf forms of many genera have a stilted, artificial appearance. A peat garden demands those that are naturally small and in which all parts of the plant are in proportion with one another. While purists may disagree, I believe that the heaths and heathers provide some of the most useful plants for filling this role. From being traditional plants of moorland and hilltop, in their modern refined forms they are very well suited to the peat garden, providing a range of colours, foliage and habit rarely found in any other acid-loving group of plants. Some traditions should be broken; one of them is that heaths and heathers should be excluded from a peat garden. However, no peat garden should be devoted exclusively to these plants.

■ *Heaths and heathers*
There are three distinct genera of plants embraced by the popular names heath and heather. The true heather or ling is *Calluna vulgaris*, the only species of the genus *Calluna*, but one which has given us a group of plants of wide variety, habit, form and colour. Heaths are represented in the main by *Erica*, but *Daboecia* is also included. There are a large number of erica species, many

A shady stream heavily planted with ostrich fern emerges into a sunny patch with primulas and skunk cabbage.

from southern Africa which are not capable of cultivation in the open in the British Isles, but the European kinds have given us a tremendous diversity for most soils and situations. *Daboecia* is commonly represented by the Irish St. Dabeoc's heath, *Daboecia cantabrica*, a more substantial plant than its contemporaries, with oval green leaves backed with silver, on stems that sport racemes of large rose-purple bell-shaped flowers. All three genera are predominantly lime-haters which prefer a free-draining soil in the open, although I have seen the common *Calluna vulgaris* growing under quite wet and shaded conditions in the wilds of northern Europe.

Erica carnea is one of the most popular species, not just because it is tolerant of difficult soil conditions, but because it comes in a wide range of colours and produces its flowers in the depths of winter. Compared with most other ericas it is well behaved, forming neat mounds of foliage, provided that it is trimmed with a pair of shears immediately after flowering. Indeed, it is important for all heaths and heathers that old flowers are cut off before new growth commences. Afterwards a handful of bonemeal into the centre of the plant is beneficial in sustaining healthy growth. There are a whole host of cultivars of *E. carnea*, but for good solid growth the vigorous sprawling 'Springwood White' and 'Springwood Pink' are amongst the best, along with the aptly named 'Pink Spangles'. These start to flower from Christmas time and will often continue until late spring.

Where a more modest habit is required, then 'King George' – some nurseries now call this 'Winter Beauty' – and 'December Red' are ideal. These start to flower earlier, and are both of a deep red colour. Foliage contrast can be provided by 'Aurea', a bushy spreading plant with golden foliage tipped with orange. It has pink flowers during the winter, but these are nothing to get very excited about.

□ Winter-flowering heaths □

For the best winter flowers we have to depend upon cultivars of *E. darleyensis*, itself a hybrid resulting from a union between *E. carnea* and the shrubby *E. mediterranea*: the pure white 'Silberschmelze', pale pink, 'Darley Dale' and red flowered 'Arthur Johnson'. All *E. darleyensis* cultivars flower throughout the winter and have tufted, bristly hummocks of foliage smothered in blossoms. Although superior garden plants to *E. carnea*, they cannot offer the diversity of colour and habit of cultivars of that species.

□ Summer-flowering heaths □

Erica cinerea is a popular summer flowering heath, a native species which has yielded all manner of colourful forms. 'C.D. Eason' has deep pink flowers; a striking contrast to the snowy-white blossoms of 'Domino'. Both are excellent flat growing kinds that form a neat carpet. So does 'P.S. Patrick', a wiry fellow with rich purple blossoms. 'Velvet Night' is a deep port wine colour, while 'Eden Valley' has flowers of soft lavender-pink. Foliage interest can be created with 'Golden Drop'. This rarely flowers, but has attractive golden leaves that turn coppery-red in the autumn. A similar proposition to the bright yellow 'Golden Hue'.

The Cornish heath, *E. vagans*, concentrates upon quantity of blossoms to attract attention. This it certainly does with cultivars like the white 'Lyonesse' and the deep cerise 'Mrs. D.F. Maxwell'. Flowering from late summer into the autumn, they sport thick bottlebrush-like flower heads in profusion. Careful pruning after flowering to remove the flowerheads is essential to maintain their shape and prevent them from becoming woody. This is not so much a problem with the cross-leaved heather, *E. tetralix* and its progeny, for its growth is softer and more graceful. An attractive subject for the summer garden, it is intolerant of wet or cold clay soil conditions and is seen at its finest in the peat garden. 'Con Underwood' has pleasing crimson flowers and mounds of delicate grey foliage, while 'Alba Mollis' offers similar attributes, but with pure white blossoms. *Erica watsonii* is a hybrid between the common *E. tetralix* and the Dorset heath, *E. ciliaris*. In its original form it is known as 'Truro', a rather mundane rose-pink plant which flowers during late summer and early autumn. However, for a really special show try 'Dawn', a beautiful foliage variety with bold rose-pink flowers that often persist until winter.

I have already mentioned fleetingly the other heaths, *Daboecia*; a small genus of dwarf shrubs, of which *D. cantabrica* is the only one of horticultural significance. A commendable plant in its own right, it has yielded some very fine cultivars. The pure white flowered 'Alba' is first class, but I love the rich purple-red flowers of 'Atropurpurea' and I am always held fascinated by the strange mixed hues of the blossoms of 'Bicolor'. Not associating too well in other parts of the garden, daboecias are useful as background plants for the peat garden. Indeed the best place for daboecias is a raised peat bed or terrace where their graceful blossoms can be more readily enjoyed at a more convenient height.

Calluna vulgaris is the common moorland heather, a variable character, which in certain selections is worth growing in the garden in its original form. There are, of course, numerous really first class varieties. Over the years many selections have been made and now the range available is so enormous that it is difficult to know where to begin. Nurserymen generally sell the ones that look best when grown in pots, but these are not necessarily the ideal varieties for a garden. When making a choice I would always include the double flowered, icing sugar-pink 'H.E. Beale' and the outstanding double, deep pink 'Peter Sparkes'. Some of the very attractive downy foliage sorts, like 'Sister Anne' and 'Silver Queen' are difficult on wet soils, but prosper in the peat garden. 'Robert Chapman' does well anywhere and is the most popular of the golden leafed heathers. There are many white flowered varieties, but if you have limited space, the dwarf 'Alba Minor' is superb. For a more conventional white, then try the natural variant called *C. vulgaris alba*. This is the lucky white heather of Scotland and has a charm all of its own. Heathers can be grown that will flower from mid-summer until early winter with the careful selection of varieties. The red flowered 'Alportii Praecox' will start to show colour during early summer, while the pale pink 'Durfordii' will rarely condescend to open until the autumn, although it will sometimes flower until Christmas if the weather remains open.

■ *Purchasing plants*
Heaths and heathers are usually purchased in pots. This is ideal providing that the plants are in good condition. So often you see weary specimens offered in moss covered pots and these are very difficult to coax into satisfactory plants. Equally it is common to see fresh bright plants in the garden centre that have obviously just emerged from a polythene tunnel. These are lush and soft and

will often rot off once planted out. Planting can be undertaken at any season of the year, but spring is best. Plants put out during cold winter weather will not make any new roots until spring and are best accommodated in a frame until then.

■ *Rhododendrons*

The same applies if you purchase young plants of rhododendron, and I suggest that you do. Large woody specimens are out of keeping in a peat garden. It is preferable to grow only small-leafed, dwarf kinds, and to prune them regularly to keep them within bounds. No peat garden is complete without these evergreen lovelies which associate so happily with heaths and heathers. Indeed, they belong to the same family and demand comparable growing conditions – a cool, moist acid soil.

Some gardeners like to grow dwarf rhododendrons that are effectively scaled down versions of the popular large flowered hybrids: vivid characters like 'Scarlet Wonder' and 'Elisabeth Hobbie'. Both are splendid plants, but a bit brash and vulgar for the peat garden. A more pleasing effect can be contrived with dwarfs like 'Blue Tit', 'Blue Diamond' and 'Yellow Hammer'. The names indicate the colours of the blossoms which are not big bold trumpets, but more refined papery flowers, that ooze quality and distinction. The most outstanding of all these dwarf small-leafed kinds is the canary yellow 'Chikor' which is marvellous when associated with the tiny 'Pink Drift' and the tight growing *Rhododendron impeditum*. This latter I find ideal for planting close to the edge of the walling so that it colonizes the blocks and provides a bold evergreen thread through the garden to hold it together visually, a factor almost as important as the background.

■ *Gaultherias*

Gaultherias are equally important for both purposes, but care has to be taken when choosing particular species, because some have a great love for peat and invade the garden completely. Never use *Gaultheria shallon* for example, not even as a background plant, as it will take over the whole neighbourhood in short order. The modest *G. miqueliana* and *G. cuneata* are different propositions, both yielding attractive pinkish fruits and having handsome evergreen foliage. The best of all, though, is *G. nummularioides*, a fine scrambling plant that makes a tough mat of foliage and is excellent for binding peat walling together.

■ *Ledums*

Other acid loving shrubby plants that rest easy in the peat garden include the ledums, phyllodoces and cassiopes. Really tough characters that are excellent for the peat garden. Most gardeners find the Labrador tea, *Ledum groenlandicum*, to be an acquired taste, for this rhododendron-like plant, with its fine evergreen foliage, is somewhat rangy and prone to untidiness. Regular surgery with the shears will keep it within bounds, so that it then yields up its creamy white flowers over a neat, tight mound. There is a compact form called 'Compactum' that will do the job for you, but this is not too readily available.

The well kept lawn is a perfect foil for this attractive planting. The striking variegated leaves of the yellow flag provide a startling contrast.

■ *Cassiopes*

Cassiopes are often referred to as North American heathers, but I find them less pleasing than our native calluna. They are nevertheless interesting small shrubs for the peat garden with thick whip-cord stems and pretty bell-like flowers. *Cassiope* 'Edinburgh' is the easiest and loveliest, with slender dark green stems and pendant blossoms of white edged with red. 'Randle Cooke' forms a tight mat from which pure white bells emerge on slender green stems while the tiny 'Muirhead' delights with curved forked shoots sprinkled in spring with nodding white flowers.

■ *Phyllodoces*

Phyllodoces have not yielded up so many fine cultivars, but their plentiful species do a good job. The widest cultivated is *Phyllodoce empetriformis*, a short tufted character with reddish-purple thimble-like flowers produced during spring. A hybrid between this and the rarely cultivated *P. glandulifera* is often encountered. Referred to as *P.* × *intermedia*, it is most commonly sold in its selection 'Fred Stoker'. This has all the qualities of *P. empetriformis*, but slightly larger urn-shaped flowers which are puckered at the mouth.

□ Peat loving favourites □

There are so many plants that qualify as favourites for the peat garden that the review which I am about to undertake will have a strong personal flavour. I will attempt to include all those that are favourites among gardeners even when they are not my own first choice. Difficulties do not arise at the outset though, for my first choice should be in everyone's collection.

■ *Meconopsis*

I have never found any gardener who is not in love with *Meconopsis betonicifolia* – the famous blue poppy of the Himalayas. A delight to the eye, but a devil to cultivate. A stately plant with rosettes of hairy plain green foliage and erect stems which support nodding saucer-shaped blossoms of the most brilliant blue. The petals are like tissue paper, but with the texture of silk, and surround a contrasting boss of rich golden stamens. They are borne in profusion during early summer, often so many blossoms being produced that the plant dies of exhaustion. Therefore it is always essential to have a few young plants standing by to make good the inevitable losses. This is easier said than done for meconopsis, like most of Nature's treasures, is notoriously difficult to grow from seed to maturity.

GROWING FROM SEED   It is generally conceded that fresh seed sown immediately it ripens is the surest way to obtain a satisfactory level of germination. This is all very well if flowering plants are to hand, but of little consolation when you are dependent upon the seedsman. Sometimes the current season's seed becomes available during late summer. This presents even greater problems. If sown in its fresh state it should germinate freely, but the plants may be difficult to over-winter. Conversely, if left until the spring viability will be lost, although the plants that result will be quite easy to bring to maturity. Seed that has not been sown shortly after ripening will generally be reluctant to germinate. However, if sown in the usual way and placed in the freezing compartment of the refrigerator for a week or ten days to give it an artificial winter, once returned to more congenial growing conditions it will germinate freely.

Getting the seedlings to emerge is one thing, rearing them to maturity is quite another. In all stages of growth meconopsis should have a moist acid compost. I like to use lime-free soilless compost, sowing the seeds on the surface and never allowing them to dry out. The seedlings should be pricked out as soon as they can be handled. The moist acid conditions which are so conducive to their germination also encourage the proliferation of choking mosses and liverworts. Having become established in a seed tray they can then be potted individually, care being taken to see that they are kept moist at all times, but never waterlogged. Shade is also important and must be provided throughout their life.

Cultivation and propagation present few problems if you fancy growing the Welsh poppy, *M. cambrica*, for this has a tendency to seed itself freely and quickly from large colonies, especially when provided with amenable damp peaty soil conditions. Ordinary *M. cambrica* has single orange or yellow flowers which are produced throughout the summer, but there are double forms too. No more than 60 cm (2 ft) high, it covers the soil with deeply cut pale green foliage. Seed sown during early spring flowers the same year.

Most meconopsis are not as agreeable in their requirements as the Welsh poppy, the majority showing more of an affinity with the more challenging *M. betonicifolia*; bold characters like the Tibetan poppy, *M. grandis*, another glory of the peat garden. A reliable perennial some 90 cm (3 ft) high, it has beautiful papery blossoms of purple or deep blue with conspicuous central clusters of creamy stamens. Its foliage is rather coarse and uninspiring, being pale green, more or less lance-shaped, and smothered in fine reddish bristles. Some gardeners confuse this with the popular *M. napaulensis*, a gorgeous peat and shade lover with papery blossoms of blue, red or maroon. It is unfortunately a monocarpic species, which means that it grows until of flowering size, blossoms, and then dies. Fortunately the deep claret *M. horridula*, yellow flowered *M. dhwojii* and bright golden *M. regia* with its magnificent over-wintering rosettes of hairy foliage, are more permanent, but it is always wise to have a few young plants of each in reserve.

■ Hellebores

The hellebores are a very different proposition, for although they take some time to become established, they are a reliable feature of the peat garden. Not exclusively plants for such a situation, it is in the damp peaty soil of a peat garden that they are their happiest. I would certainly never consider my garden complete without one or two clumps, for they are amongst the most useful plants for winter decoration in the peat garden. With their attractive waxen blossoms and bold mounds of handsome foliage, they stand defiant against hostile weather that sweeps almost everything else away.

The hellebores are divided into two distinct groups: the caulescent species such as *Helleborus argutifolius* and *H. foetidus* which have annual stems surmounted by flowers, and the stemless or acaulescent kinds which include *H. niger* and *H. atrorubens*. The former group is quite small and apart from those species mentioned, only *H. lividus* is of any consequence to the gardener. This is actually regarded by many as a sub-species of *H. argutifolius*, a plant which it resembles in almost everything except stature. An easy-going fellow, *H. lividus* produces short flower stems no more than 30 cm (1 ft) high and marbled foliage with purplish undersides. This dark infusion spreads to the attractive greenish blossoms which are produced during late winter and early spring. Of course most gardeners are familiar with *H. argutifolius* by sight if not by name, for this is the plant which until recent years was known as *H. corsicus*, an excellent plant with tall cane-like stems and expansive serrated leaves and apple-green flowers. It can be somewhat vigorous for the smaller peat garden, but where this is the case then try its progeny *H. × sternii*. This is the result of a union between *H. argutifolius* and *H. lividus*, and presents the best of both parents in selected stock. Unfortunately there appears to be a number of inferior kinds about which are not worthy of cultivation, but the typical hybrid with large soft green blossoms infused with purple which are held above attractively marbled foliage, is most desirable and well suited to the peat garden. The stinking hellebore, *H. foetidus*, is also amenable to such a life, producing mounds of beautifully cut dark green foliage and contrasting heads of pendulous apple-green blossoms during early spring. Although a native, it is not to be despised, for it is one of the loveliest plants for a shaded corner, particularly if there is a tendency to dry out, for it will tolerate fluctuations in moisture level much better than most other peat lovers.

The Christmas rose, *H. niger*, is undoubtedly the best known member of the family. Flowering from early winter until the early spring, it sports characteristic icy-white saucer-shaped blossoms with central clusters of lemon stamens. These are borne singly on stout stems which arise from amidst attractive glossy evergreen foliage. Numerous forms exist, but *H. niger* var. *macranthus* is in my opinion still the finest. This has typical divided foliage with a somewhat bluish tinge and large white blooms devoid of the pinkish suffusion which invades the petals of most commercial forms and cutivars. The plants are neat and compact and well suited to the small peat garden. *Helleborus atrorubens* flowers about the same time as the Christmas rose and indeed was once erroneously called *H. niger* var. *roseus*. It is a handsome species of similar character to *H. niger*, but with variable palmate leaves that are not reliably evergreen, and handsome blossoms of deep maroon with a distinct violet tinge. The delicate pendant blooms of *H. abchasicus* are of similar hue and produced amongst foliage that often shows a reddish infusion. Together with *H. atrorubens* and the sweetly scented yellowish-green flowered *H. odorus*, this forms a trio of the most frequent parents of that horticulturally invaluable group, the Lenten roses. Flowering somewhat later than many of their cousins, this collective group of hybrids embraces the entire colour range exhibited by the helleborus species and includes a number of interesting additional shades. The true *H. orientalis* only superficially resembles the Lenten roses, having larger creamy-white blossoms which age to brown and expansive palmate evergreen foliage.

Of the green flowered species the most useful for the peat garden is our native *H. viridis*. This has attractive olive-green foliage which dies away during the winter, reappearing again in early spring together with pendant clusters of small cup-shaped blossoms of soft apple-green. These are slightly malodorous, but not offensive, and remain in character for a number of weeks. Like most of the hellebores it can be raised from seed, but care must be taken to see that seed is collected from suitably protected blossoms or cross pollination with

Access to the water enables the plantings to be viewed from a completely different angle and permits exploitation of the water's reflective qualities.

other species will occur. Seed should always be sown immediately it ripens for then germination will occur in a matter of weeks. Older seed remains viable, but is very difficult to induce into growth and must often remain sown for a year or more before any activity is observed. Of course division can be resorted to, despite the uncompromising nature of the helleborus rootstock. This is best done during late summer just prior to renewed root activity, the plants being divided into quite small portions and lined out in a frame. Care must be taken to see that they never dry out as initially they only have a tenuous hold upon life. This is gradually strengthened as the weeks pass by and within nine months they are self supporting and ready to plant out.

Another delightful harbinger of spring is the lovely little *Hepatica nobilis*, for apart from the early bulbs there is nothing to compare with this little gem for freedom of flowering and intensity of colour. Doubtless still known to many as *Anemone hepatica*, its initial appearance does show a certain affinity with that genus, however its leaves are quite distinctly heart-shaped and bluntly three-lobed. The dainty blue flowers are like soft silky stars and borne in profusion on wiry stems that arise from clumps of attractive apple-green foliage. When flowering commences during early New Year these are mere wisps of downy green, but as the last flowers fade during the rapidly lengthening days of late spring they have erupted into mounds of cheerful bright green foliage. Hepaticas are at their happiest revelling in a cool deep soil well laced with peat, but need constant protection from the attention of slugs which are sometimes a nuisance, damaging the young flower buds as they push through the soil. Apart from the common species there is a white cultivar *H. n.* 'Alba' as well as the pink and mauve varieties *H. n.* 'Rosea' and *H. n.* 'Lilacina', although the latter are currently difficult to find.

■ *Hardy gingers*

The hardy gingers or roscoeas are becoming easier to get hold of, and it is about time too; the nursery trade has been very slow to promote these gorgeous confidence tricksters. Their exotic orchid-like blossoms suggest that they might be extremely difficult to grow successfully, but they are in fact very easy. There are four species which are hardy, but only two are really outstanding: *Roscoea humeana* and *R. cautleoides*. Both are natives of western China and have characteristic sheaths of light green lanceolate foliage which embrace clusters of startling blossoms. These are quaintly hooded and each has two pendant lateral lobes which give the blooms an undeniable tropical appearance. In *R. humeana* they are rich rosy-purple, while in *R. cautleoides* they are pale sulphurous yellow. Neither species grows more than 30 cm (1 ft) high and both are at their best in the peat garden, though they are happy in a rock garden pocket in suitable soil.

■ *Lilies*

So are most of the lilies. While they can be offered a place in the open ground, the majority grow so much better in the peat garden if a little sharp grit is added to improve the drainage. Lilies are, of course, the queens of the summer garden. Brightly coloured and with exotic blossoms, they are often mistakenly thought to be difficult by new gardeners. While it is true that there are a few fickle kinds, most of those that are popularly available from nurseries and garden centres are easy-going and reliable if provided with the kind of conditions afforded by a peat garden. There are many varieties to choose from, but it is generally conceded that the Mid-Century hybrids embrace those of easiest cultivation and greatest versatility. Making a recommendation is very much a personal fancy. While I realize that the nasturtium-red 'Enchantment' is seen in almost every modern garden where lilies are grown, it is nevertheless one of the most reliable and would receive my vote as the perfect lily for the beginner, closely followed by the deep lemon-yellow 'Destiny'. All the Mid-Century hybrids are robust lilies with strong flower stems that rarely need supporting.

Others are not quite so versatile, but much more spectacular, especially the golden-rayed lily of Japan, *Lilium auratum*, and the regal lily, *L. regale*. Both have magnificent trumpet-shaped blossoms in white and gold with a rich heady fragrance. Although enjoying life in a moist peaty medium, they need careful placing towards the back if they are not to dominate the feature by reason of their size and exotic appearance.

A favourite from days gone by is the orange flowered tiger lily, *L. tigrinum*. Now greatly improved by selection, this hardy old-timer is joined by various hybrids and colour variants, including a rather fine yellow form known as *flavum* or *flaviflorum*. *Lilium speciosum* and its varieties *rubrum* and *magnificum* extend the flowering season well into autumn. All have lovely waxy pendant blossoms in various shades and combinations of crimson and white, the stately *L. henryi* with finely sculptured glowing orange blossoms and the shorter growing *L. martagon*, blossoms of purple-maroon. The majority of lilies prefer a free-draining medium of acid persuasion, and benefit from a generous quantity of sharp sand or grit incorporating into the soil before planting. It is also prudent to sprinkle a little sand in the bottom of each planting hole for the bulbs to rest on. This not only benefits drainage, but encourages rapid root development as well. If your soil is not in a good condition at planting time it is better to start the bulbs in a soilless potting compost in pots, moving them to their permanent positions when they are actively growing and outdoor conditions have improved.

When choosing lily bulbs, take great care. Unlike most other bulbous plants they are extremely fleshy and very vulnerable to drying out. Responsible nurserymen will always keep lily bulbs in boxes of sawdust and peat and not permit their exposure to the air. Unlike many other packaged plants, lilies are well suited to display in polythene pre-packs as the air cannot dry them out so readily. However, they must still be kept under cool conditions to prevent premature sprouting. Never be tempted by lilies that have developed shoots, for they rarely produce a satisfactory display the first year. In general, lilies are easy-going and demand little attention. They suffer few ailments either, especially when growing in a well ordered garden.

The only problem that the gardener should be vigilant about is virus disease. This is not an infrequent occurrence and causes the development of stunted, distorted foliage and twisted flowers, or in extreme cases the complete absence of blossoms. Regrettably there is no cure, so diseased plants must be dug up and thrown on the bonfire. If you only purchase quality bulbs from a reliable source, then the likelihood of introducing virus is fairly remote. Unfortunately virus diseases do not respect garden boundaries, and it is from neighbouring gardens that infection is most likely to come. So look out for greenfly which transmit the disease while feeding on the sap, and endeavour to keep these under control by spraying regularly with a systemic insecticide throughout the summer.

■ *Aroids*

Before moving on from bulbous plants I must mention some of the most interesting and curious plants that the peat gardener can grow, the moisture-loving hardy aroids, members of the arum family. I have earlier mentioned the skunk cabbages or lysichitons with their bold spathes. The arisaemas are somewhat similar, but much smaller and on a taller stem. The best known species is *Arisaema triphyllum*, a native of North America which is popularly called Jack-in-the-pulpit, a name which arises from the curious form and positioning of the spathe and spadix. The quaintly hooded inflorescences, varying in colour from pale green to dark purple, are borne above trifoliate foliage during early summer and followed in the autumn by bright scarlet berries. *Arisaema candidissimum* grows in similar fashion, but sports whitish spathes tinged with rose and makes an excellent companion in a shady situation.

The true arums are also appreciative of shaded conditions in a richly organic medium, a fact well endorsed by our native cuckoo pint, *Arum maculatum*.

Opposite: *A carefully planted streamside incorporating blue Siberian iris, variegated flag and the creamy-flowered* Trollius *or globe flower.*
Below: *This stream entices the visitor to follow its path through the garden. Instead of dividing the garden, it serves as its axis.*

Although seldom cultivated, it is not without character, but where space is at a premium it is better replaced by *A. italicum*. This is a small robust perennial with creamy-white spathes and a host of glossy green arrow-shaped foliage interspersed in the autumn with stout spikes of rich red berries. A much improved form, *A. italicum* var. *marmoratum*, has beautiful dark green foliage marbled with yellow and is punctuated freely with sprays of vermilion fruits. *Arum dioscoridis* is not quite so resilient, needing to become established in a sheltered situation before thrusting up its fine violet and black marbled spathes on short stout flower stems. The type usually seen in gardens is *A. dioscoridis* var. *smithii*, an altogether more desirable plant with large hastate leaves and flowers more deeply etched with black. A complete contrast is provided by *A. crinitum*, a grotesque plant with gaping purplish spathes four or five inches wide and long spadices covered with reddish-purple hairs. The inflorescence as a whole emits an offensive odour, which no doubt accounts for its lack of popularity amongst conventional gardeners.

■ *Wood lilies*
None of the wood lilies or trilliums suffers this handicap, for all are beautiful and much loved by gardeners everywhere. The wake robin, *Trillium grandiflorum*, is undoubtedly the finest, a splendid fellow with large three-petalled snowy-white blossoms above handsome fresh green foliage. There are also rose-pink and green flowered forms that enthusiasts crave for, but these are of little decorative merit. When a pink kind is wanted, *T. stylosum* will oblige, while *T. sessile* will provide smaller flowers of deep crimson and var. *luteum* those of lemon-yellow. *Trillium erectum* is very variable and embraces a colour range that extends from white to deep mahogany and the aptly named painted trillium, *T. undulatum*, has pure white blossoms splashed and stained with red.

■ *Bloodroot*
Merely mentioning trillium brings to mind sanguinaria, for this little gem thrives in the same conditions and like the trilliums grows from a thick fleshy rhizome. The North American bloodroot, *Sanguinaria canadensis*, is a peach of a plant with grey-green kidney-shaped leaves and solitary white flowers like snowy goblets. The fully double form var. *multiplex* is even more striking, and although usually considered to be a specialist's plant, is in actual fact no more difficult to grow than its less sophisticated brother if provided with damp peaty soil and a little shade. The only problem that I have encountered is the persistent attacks made by wood pigeons upon dormant rhizomes. For some inexplicable reason they home in on any plants that are not suitably protected.

■ *Rodgersias*
Rodgersias I always consider to be rather special. Even though they are not suitable for the smaller peat garden, they can make a contribution elsewhere if you provide them with a rich peaty medium. Of all the lovely plants which we grow in our gardens, one of the most regularly badly grown groups is the rodgersias. Except when growing in very peaty conditions their foliage looks dull and tedious, often with crumbling brown edges. When grown well though, they are a delight, especially *Rodgersia tabularis* with its handsome circular fresh green leaves. This is the odd species out, for all the others have bold divided foliage, that of *R. aesculifolia* looking rather like a horse chestnut's.

However, their crowded heads of frothy flowers show their close affinity to the astilbe, and in most cases are a creamy-white colour or tinged with pink and have a subtle musky fragrance. All have thick, knobbly, clump forming rootstocks that separate easily for propagation.

□ Little gems □

Separating plants from within the extensive range of peat lovers and highlighting some of the rarer and more difficult varieties is perhaps a dubious exercise. For some gardeners find one to be more difficult than another, and availability is a variable that modern propagation techniques have now revolutionized. Nevertheless there are some scarce peat lovers that demand star treatment, for they are of exceptional merit, and while not always being the most beautiful plants around, they present a challenge that appeals to the true plantsman. Top of the list must be the beautiful hardy lady's slipper orchids. The extremely rare lady's slipper, *Cypripedium calceolus*, is well known, but there are a number of other gorgeous species that are very hardy and can be grown successfully in a cool moist peaty soil. The North American *C. reginae*, with its delectable pouched blossoms of pink and white, and that little pink flowered beauty *C. acaule*. *Cypripedium pubescens* has large yellow and brown blooms like those of *C. calceolus*, but on taller stems. Indeed, this is sometimes classified as a variety of *C. calceolus*. But the most startling of all is the oriental *C. japonicum* with greenish-white flowers flushed and splashed with crimson. The orchis or dactylorchis as we should perhaps call them are also striking, especially the tall purple flowered *Dactylorchis elata*, one of the best of these hardy orchids for the peat garden. With stems up to 90 cm (3 ft) high, it is one of the most remarkable members of the orchid family. While many of the other orchis are reasonably freely available, it is only this and the similar paler purple flowered *Dactylorchis maderensis* that you should consider. Most of the other species are more meadow-land plants.

Another group of plants which command instant attention are the may apples, curious members of the berberis family with quaint parasol-like foliage. They are easily raised from seed and are ready for planting during their second year. Two species are cultivated, the North American *Podophyllum peltatum* and the Himalayan *P. emodi*. The latter is the most striking, with bronze, purple and green mottled foliage and dainty white or soft rose saucer-shaped blossoms. These are followed by large crimson tomato-like seed pods which remain in character for much of the winter. *Podophyllum peltatum* is of similar habit, but with soft green foliage and pure white flowers followed by fruits of a reddish-orange hue. The umbrella leaf, *Diphylleia cymosa*, is closely related and like its cousins produces attractive silvery-white flowers during late spring. These are borne in terminal heads above expansive fresh green foliage and give way in the autumn to brilliant blue berries that are the equal of any produced by *Viburnum davidii*.

Of course not all plants can provide the combination of attractive foliage, flower and fruit offered by the preceding, but some like the Chinese poppy, *Eomecon chionantha*, possess at least two of these qualities. Although not exclusively a shade lover, eomecon produces its finest foliage when out of the sun. This is somewhat rounded and of a metallic hue and borne on stems the colour of rich caramel. Paper white blossoms are in evidence throughout the summer, sprinkled amongst the foliage like fallen cherry blossom after a spring shower. In moist peaty conditions it grows freely and may need gently controlling.

■ *Primulas*

It is not my role here to point gardeners in the direction of the impossible, but we cannot leave the peat garden without mentioning primulas. A number of the moisture-loving kinds that I have already discussed, such as *Primula waltoni*, *P. sikkimensis* and *P. viali* are all at home in the peat garden and can make a considerable contribution to it, but there are one or two specials for which most gardeners yearn. For me it is the wonderful *P. bhutanica*, a gem of a plant which I have loved and lost on the edge of peat walling a number of times. It needs moisture, yet must be free-draining and for winter protection should have a sheet of glass raised over the crowns. Any attention is well rewarded, for it produces the most exquisite heads of icy-blue blossoms during early spring when the rest of the garden is just awakening. If you are not so confident about tackling *P. bhutanica*, then try some of the *P. sieboldii* hybrids. These are beautiful plants in shades of pink and rose through to white, with neatly scalloped pale green leaves. Not the easiest of primulas, but they are fairly responsive to life in the peat garden and make a lovely show each year during late spring.

□ Maintenance □

It is very easy to wax lyrical over all these plants, but I have given precious little guidance as to how to maintain them! Looking after plants in a peat garden is very similar to those that are grown elsewhere. Weeds can be a nuisance, particularly hairy bitter cress with its dull green divided leaves, small white flowers and explosive seed pods. This is a common weed in any soil where there is a generous amount of peat. Willow and birch seedlings frequently appear in peaty mediums and these should be removed as soon as noticed. Do not be tempted to plant them elsewhere in the garden as they are likely to be of inferior hybrid forms. Regular weeding is the key to success, for the growing medium in a peat garden is well suited to most weeds, particularly those that spread by means of underground rootstocks. Once couch grass, bindweed or perennial nettles become established in a peat garden, it is a case of demolishing it and starting again.

Many of the peat-loving plants are also vigorous growers, so these should be planted where they will cause least competition, especially where you consider establishing some of my little gems. Remember too, that no one form of gardening is the preserve of any one plant, except in exceptional circumstances. While I have indicated a number of the popular plants which I would include, there are at least as many of equal worth which I have left out. As I indicated at the beginning this is my personal review of plants that I think you will enjoy. When planning your own feature include a fern or two, for although I have treated these lovely foliage plants separately, they too have an important role to play in most peat gardens.

Trollius or globe flowers are amongst the earliest streamside plants to flower and continue into summer.

CHAPTER SEVEN

FERNS AND MOSSES

There cannot be a group of plants more neglected and maligned than the ferns and mosses. Few gardens would not be improved by these amenable plants, yet since the great Victorian fern era they have slipped into relative obscurity. Although many of the extremely fine named varieties of ferns that were grown by our grandparents were lost during the neglect of the First World War, there is still sufficient diversity around to enable the imaginative gardener to create a picture of cool green beauty, especially if he introduces some of the easily grown mosses.

□ The fernery □

Victorian gardeners used to create areas of the garden where nothing but ferns and mosses were allowed to grow. In modern gardens the creation of a fernery is an extravagance that few of us can afford, so ferns are either integrated into the general garden scene or planted in their own shaded border – what one today could perhaps term the modern fernery.

Unquestionably ferns look more pleasing when grown in harmony alongside one another, mosses providing a low green foil and obscuring the soil. Treat them along similar lines to herbaceous plants, but feed sparingly and do not divide clumps as regularly and vigorously as you might for delphiniums, michaelmas daisies or golden rod. Choose a partially shaded site with preferably a northerly aspect, ideally on soil of medium loam. Free draining sandy soils and heavy uncompromising clays are difficult to deal with, few ferns or mosses prospering under such hostile conditions. Moisture is obviously important for both ferns and mosses, but it should not be so damp that it becomes stale and stagnant. All soils benefit from the inclusion of well rotted animal manure, leaf mould, or coarse moss peat dug well in during early autumn. If the upturned soil can be left to the mercy of the elements, it will be in ideal condition for planting during the following spring. Although ferns can be planted at any time from early autumn until spring, it is just as they are moving into growth that they transplant most successfully.

Routine care of a modern fernery consists of controlling weeds and mulching those ferns that demand constant moisture. There are ferns that grow best in rock work and these require similar conditions, but benefit from top dressing with grit. They are the smaller kinds which, while needing dampness, do not enjoy sitting in the wet, nor prosper with an organic mulch around their crowns. A generous layer of grit does conserve moisture, but prevents the rotting of the plants. To ensure ideal conditions for these delightful little fellows it is prudent to remove a generous quantity of soil and place a layer of clinker or coarse gravel in the bottom of the hole. The soil that has been removed can then be mixed with sharp lime-free grit at approximately one part grit to five of soil by volume and then replaced.

Management of a fern and moss collection is not arduous. Good garden hygiene, including the regular removal of fading foliage is all that is required. If you wish to grow really fine specimen plants of ferns rather than just create a blending of foliage, it is necessary to employ what is called the single crown method of culture. This means that the fern is restricted to one centre of growth and not permitted to form a crowd of offsets. The 'shuttlecock' ferns, that is those that form a circle of fronds around a central basal stem, are very proficient at producing young plants around the bases of mature fronds. If left to their own devices they rapidly assume adult proportions and in doing so jostle for light, air and root run. This invariably results in the plants becoming dwarfed while the crowding of the foliage detracts from the grace and beauty of the individual. A single crown, kept so by the persistent removal of such progeny will have fronds of much greater stature and show off its form and habit to better advantage.

□ Dependable ferns □

The toughest and easiest ferns to grow are the buckler ferns. These are part of the genus *Dryopteris* and include familiar characters like the male fern, *D. filix-mas*, a coarse growing plant of dignified stature, attaining a height of some 90 cm–1.2 m (3–4 ft) under favourable conditions. It has lance-shaped fresh green fronds which emerge during early spring from a large woody rootstock. They are often clothed with rust coloured protective scales which persist for much of the summer. Although growing happily anywhere, the male fern much prefers a moist leafy soil in partial shade.

Garden forms of the common male fern are numerous and exhibit such bizarre and complex frond mutations as to be totally unrecognizable as derivations from such an uncomplicated parent. The most outstanding is unquestionably *D. f. m.* 'Grandiceps'. The fronds of this plant resemble those of the common male fern in texture, colour and stature, but are bedecked at their tips with heavy tassels of crested leaflets. A form known as *D. f. m.* 'Grandiceps Wills' is sometimes grown, and can be easily distinguished by the enormous much branched crests, which weigh heavily on the tall resplendent fronds.

Dryopteris f. m. 'Polydactyla' is of similar aspect, producing short narrow fronds which rarely exceed 45 cm (1 ft 6 in) in height. The tips are divided into very brittle finger-like crests which, instead of taking a typical pendant poise, remain stiffly straight and erect. In well-grown plants the fronds are dark olive-green, but seem only to attain this colour when pot grown. For some unaccountable reason open ground plants develop a type of chlorosis, which shows as a fine green mottling on a pale yellow background. The plants do not seem to suffer unduly from this disorder, but nevertheless look unfit when seen intermingled with the bright green foliage of other hardy dryopteris. This is not a problem with *D. f. m.* 'Cristata', a plant of exceptional merit with attractive crested leaflets. There are several distinct forms, two of the most

popular being *D. f. m.* 'Cristata Jackson' with tall, heavily crested, fronds some 90 cm (3 ft) high and *D. f. m.* 'Cristata Martindale' with decumbent leaflets bending towards the frond tips. Both are first class garden plants, far superior to the common *D. f. m.* 'Cristata'.

In addition to these lovely forms there are some more unusual kinds which always demand attention. *Dryopteris f. m.* 'Barnesii', with long, narrow tapering fronds carried in an elegant arching fashion, the finely divided *D. f. m.* 'Linearis Congesta' and the exquisite plumose male fern, *D. f. m.* 'Bollandiae' which has finely dissected green feathery foliage which turns a burnished copper shade at the approach of autumn. Formerly grouped as a form of the male fern, *Dryopteris borreri* is often confused with it. However, it is quite distinct, having blunt-ended leaflets and a dense golden scaly covering to both crown and stem. This has led to its being called the golden-scaled male fern. Apart from the usual kind there is a compact crested form with heavily congested fronds called *D. b.* 'Congesta Cristata'.

■ Buckler ferns

The true buckler ferns are very tough and add interest to the garden for much of the year, being semi-evergreen and on occasions carrying their foliage through all the seasons. They adapt well to most soils and situations, although they abhor full sun and dryness at the roots. The broad buckler fern, *D. dilatata*, is a most attractive plant. An inhabitant of streamsides and water meadows, it has broadly triangular fronds 60–90 cm (2–3 ft) high which arise from a stout scaly rootstock. Prospering in damp leafy soil, it is often confused with the prickly buckler fern, *D. carthusiana*, a plant with similar requirements, but narrow fronds with distinctive spined and indented leaflets. There are no readily available garden forms of *D. carthusiana*, but with modern propagation techniques, variations of *D. dilatata*, like 'Cristata' and 'Crispa' are becoming increasingly popular.

These are of course crested and crimped foliage forms and the popular name crested buckler fern would lead you to believe that *D. cristata* which carries this name would be extensively frilled. This is not the case, for this handsome native of wet marshy ground has sturdy, pale green, divided fronds. These unfurl in the spring, the rapidly expanding leaflets below the uncoiling frond tip appearing to embrace it. A plant of acid soil, it spreads rapidly by a scaly creeping rootstock in much the same manner as the winged wood fern, *D. hexagonoptera*, a short growing North American native with delicate little triangular, divided fronds some 23 cm (9 in) high, which are carried on persistent straw-coloured stems.

■ Lady ferns

The athyriums or lady ferns are much more refined than the common buckler ferns. Indeed, for grace, elegance and tolerance of widely differing situations, few ferns can compare with the common lady fern, *Athyrium filix-femina*. This charming woodlander, with its dainty, arching, pale green fronds, has been the delight of gardeners for many years, giving rise to innumerable very distinctive and attractive varieties.

Moisture-loving plants enjoy the splash from the waterfall in this cleverly planted garden. Every nook and cranny is used to good effect.

The ordinary species is very adaptable and appears to be capable of producing frond forms compatible with the conditions under which it is growing. Indeed in some cases the differences in the structure of the fronds are so great as to mislead one into believing that they belong to plants of entirely different species. However, under conditions of partial shade and ample moisture the fronds are fairly uniform in both size and structure. They grow abundantly from a stout, tufted rootstock, are lance-shaped, very brittle, and attain a height of some 90 cm–1.2 m (3–4 ft). The long, slender frond stalks are purplish in colour and support alternate pairs of handsome velvety green leaflets. When the young fronds unfurl during late spring they are thickly clothed in deep rust-red scales and emit a sweet delightful earthy aroma. Unfortunately both of these lovely characteristics are short-lived, the aroma disappearing within a few days of the fronds unfurling, and the scales withering and dropping off after a further two or three weeks. Another shortcoming of this species is the way in which it sheds its fronds prematurely in the autumn, whether or not a frost has occurred. Almost overnight they assume a rich lemon-yellow hue and within a few days have shrivelled away completely, leaving only the tip of the brown tufted rootstock above ground.

Culture is easy. A moist position in partial shade is all they desire, together with occasional lifting and replanting of old crowns. This encourages stronger growth, for in many old plants the crown grows right out of the ground, making life extremely difficult for the young roots, therefore replanting at regular intervals helps to revitalize them by putting roots and ground in close proximity. A heavy mulch with old leaves or well-rotted manure will provide the same effect.

Towards the end of the famous Victorian fern era there were no fewer than forty distinct garden varieties of *Athyrium filix-femina* in commerce. Sadly, many of these have been lost to cultivation, but those that have survived are of sound constitution and exhibit many diverse and pleasing habits of growth. The most outstanding of these is *A. f. f.* 'Victoriae', found close on a century ago, allegedly under a hedgerow in central Scotland. This form produces fronds of a similar size and nature to those of the species, except that the leaflets are attractively crested and cross one another in an almost religiously symbolic manner. Many forms of this are currently in circulation, mostly raised from spores, but it is doubtful whether few, if any, really measure up to the excellent form exhibited by those obtained from divisions of the original find. The tatting fern, *A. f. f.* 'Frizelliae' is another extraordinary variation, this time discovered in Ireland. Attaining a height of no more than 45 cm (1 ft 6 in), in this form, the individual leaflets are reduced to curious little balls, which give the fronds a most unusual appearance. Several different and crested forms have occurred in young plants raised from spores, but on the whole, stock grown in this manner is fairly even. *Athyrium f. f.* 'Frizelliae Cristatum' is an exceptionally fine dwarf crested form of the tatting fern which is almost weighed down to the ground by its exhaustive terminal crest.

One of the most refined and graceful lady ferns is *A. f. f.* 'Multifidum'. In this the fronds are finely cut and surmounted by slender, delicately branched, finger-like crests. A contrast is provided by *A. f. f.* 'Plumosum', a slightly smaller variety with pale green, wispy, feathery fronds of exceptional beauty. Many named selections of this form are available and decidedly superior to the common sort. Spores produce interesting variations, but the best varieties are grown from divisions.

The same applies to the most bizarre lady fern of all, *A. f. f.* 'Caput Medusae', a small growing shade lover of dubious garden merit but great curiosity value with leaflets that form a tight congested ball at the top of a short, almost leafless stem.

■ *Shield ferns*

The various shield ferns also produce wide variation in habit and form, but the two common species are difficult to surpass in their unspoilt state. Although showing considerable divergence of habit amongst individuals, both the hard shield fern, *Polystichum aculeatum*, and the soft shield fern, *P. setiferum*, provide a perfect foil for more brightly coloured neighbours. The former has broad lance-shaped fronds arranged in a circular fashion around a short woody rootstock. They are dark green and leathery above, grey-green and soft beneath, and carry neat rows of spores on the undersides of the leaflets. The stalks are densely clothed in rust-coloured scales. A form known as *P. aculeatum* var. *lobatum* has narrow fronds and much larger and coarser leaflets. Both seem to do well anywhere where there are liberal amounts of moisture available.

So too, does *P. setiferum*, a very closely related species, on occasions described as a mere variation of the hard shield fern. It has pale green, much less crowded fronds, but otherwise is very similar. The rootstock is hard and woody, and covered with large brown scales which extend right up the frond stalks. These are quite flexible and no doubt account to a certain extent for the plant's common name of soft shield fern. Apart from being a most desirable acquisition in itself, *P. setiferum* has also given rise to many fine garden varieties with tasselled and much divided fronds. Probably the most popular of these is *P. s.* 'Divisilobum'. This has broad fronds consisting of a multitude of finely cut leaflets which divide at the ends into pointed finger-like projections. The fronds grow to about 60 cm (2 ft) high, are dark green, and supported on short, extremely hairy and scaly frond stalks. Two forms known as 'Divisilobum Densum' and 'Divisilobum Densum Superbum' are superior, but do not appear to be as robust or long-lived.

Another of the popular variations is *P. proliferum*, a confusing plant said by some to be a species, but generally conceded as being a form of *P. setiferum*. Whatever it is, it is one of the finest hardy ferns with spreading lacy foliage amongst which tiny plantlets are produced. If a frond is detached and pegged down in a tray of good compost, the embryo ferns will quickly root.

The hart's tongue fern, *Phyllitis scolopendrium*, has an even more ingenious method of vegetative reproduction. If healthy fronds are pulled away from the rootstock and the lower couple of centimetres detached, these will root and develop into plants when placed in a damp sandy medium, the technique being referred to as propagation by frond bases. Not that you normally need to do this for the common species with its solid, strap-like dark green, leathery fronds, for this produces quantities of viable spores. However, fancy varieties like the crested *P. s.* 'Ramo-Cristatum' and the frilled and crimpled *P. s.* 'Crispum' rarely if ever produce spores and can otherwise only be increased by division.

This is also true of the osmundas, for although they produce liberal quantities of spores, these have a very short life, their viability being little more than a few days following ripening. No self-respecting gardener in Victorian times would neglect to grow the royal fern, *Osmunda regalis*, at the waterside.

A huge dignified plant up to 1.8 m (6 ft) high, it has large leathery fronds that change colour with age from pale lime-green to rich burnished bronze. Unfortunately their glowing autumnal tints are short-lived, for the foliage is very tender, and at the first touch of frost shrivels and hangs limply from the woody semi-persistent frond stalks. Although it is completely hardy, it is advisable to cover the over-wintering crowns with a thick layer of straw or bracken to give some measure of protection to the emerging young female fronds in the spring. In addition to the ordinary species there are a number of fancy varieties, including the crested royal fern, *O. regalis* 'Cristata', in which the fronds terminate in attractive tassels of twisted leaflets, the crimped and crested *O. r.* 'Undulata' and the purple-leafed *O. r.* 'Purpurescens'.

Its cousins are not so enthusiastic about swampy conditions, although they certainly demand a damp leafy medium. Of more modest proportions with conspicuously upright fronds, they prefer a corner with dappled shade. One of my favourites is the interrupted fern, *Osmunda claytoniana*. This is a most extraordinary fellow, deriving its common name from the spores that are borne in a solid mass around the stalk in a central area of the frond which is completely devoid of leaflets. The leaflets above and below this fructification are quite normally developed, giving the entire frond the appearance of having been interrupted. The surrounding green sterile fronds are quite normal and of a soft velvety texture, making a perfect contrast for the chocolate brown fruiting body.

■ *Cinnamon fern*

The cinnamon fern, *O. cinnamomea*, is lovely too, the coppery coloured woolly growth which covers the young fronds as they emerge in the spring being one of the most striking characteristics of this species. Unfortunately this disappears long before the imposing soft green fronds have completely unfurled, but is replaced by another important feature; indeed the one to which the plant's common name alludes. In the midst of the abundant green barren fronds an occasional fertile one appears. This is stout and erect, and covered with an extensive terminal cluster of cinnamon-coloured spore-bearing bodies which gives the fruiting portion a distinctive mottled appearance. For the best results this should be planted in a rich moist leafy soil in semi-shaded conditions.

■ *Polypodies*

Not all ferns respond to such conditions, although it is true that they have a constant moisture requirement. The polypodies often cling to moss or organic debris on rock or stones, surviving for many years and reproducing freely. This is not sensible to attempt to recreate in the garden, and so free-draining soil must be provided. The best loved polypody is our native *Polypodium vulgare*, the progenitor of many interesting forms and variations. The ordinary species has coarsely divided more or less evergreen leathery fronds no more than 30 cm (1 ft) long which are produced from a slender creeping rootstock. Ideal for the rock garden, it is indifferent as to soil conditions, providing that they are well drained. Among the fancy kinds I have a strong affection for the crested

Sculpture, stone and plants are complementary. The horizontal and vertical lines of conifers and maples accentuate the oriental atmosphere.

P. v. 'Cristatum' with its semi-pendulous terminal crests and the strange *P. v.* 'Cornubiense' which has three distinct types of frond. The common kind of frond should always be removed or else the desirable portion of the plant will be overwhelmed.

■ *Spleenworts*

There are innumerable other ferns suited to rocky outcrops, but it is amongst the spleenworts that some of the best are to be found. These are the aspleniums, represented in most gardens by *Asplenium trichomanes*, the maidenhair spleenwort. Its slender arching fronds up to 15–23 cm (6–9 in) in length support legions of rounded dull green leaflets giving it the overall aspect of a maidenhair fern. The green spleenwort, *A. viride*, is very similar and was for many years believed to be a mere variant. This has attractive green stems which are more flaccid, and typical masses of small rounded leaflets. Not so *A. ruta-muraria*, the tiniest of the spleenworts and popularly known as wall rue. Tiny stiff, almost evergreen, wedge-shaped fronds arise from a short scaleless rootstock. In the wild this plant is found growing in rock crevices amongst mosses and lichens; conditions which are difficult to simulate in a garden, except possibly in a dry wall. Great success can be achieved, however, by growing this lovely little plant in a mixture of equal parts loam and peat in the holes of a common house air-brick; the brick being stood on edge so that the plants can cascade down its face and almost completely hide the brick itself from view.

■ *Bladder ferns*

The bladder ferns or cystopteris are excellent dwarf ferns for similar situations, especially in very cold areas, filling rock crevices with brittle, soft green filigree fronds. *Cystopteris fragilis* is the most endearing. A little gem with fragile, broadly lance-shaped, translucent fronds some 23 cm (9 in) high. These arise from a prostrate rootstock which is thickly covered in broad golden–brown scales. Although spores are freely produced, they are seldom used for propagation because the rootstocks are so readily divisible. Apart from the common species, there is the crested brittle bladder fern, *C. fragilis* 'Cristata', a mutant with quaintly crested leaflets. This is a real gem, which needs growing in an alpine house if one is to do it justice. Not so the berry bladder fern, *C. bulbifera*, even though it looks superficially like a larger *C. fragilis* with weak stems. This is one of the easiest dwarf ferns to grow, sporting delicate pale green fronds and scattering tiny dark green bulbils asunder. If gathered swiftly these can be planted in trays in a good free-draining potting compost and be ready for planting out in less than a year.

■ *Evergreen ferns*

Gardeners who have to contend with soil of acid persuasion should try that charming New Zealander, *Blechnum penna-marina*, a sweet little evergreen with dark rippling fronds which quickly grow into a congested patch. This is a dwarf version of the larger hard fern, *Blechnum spicant*, unquestionably the finest of the readily available evergreen ferns of moderate stature. A striking native, this has narrow dark green, leathery barren fronds 60 cm (2 ft) long. The fertile ones are slightly larger, covered in extensive fructifications and stand erect from the centre of the plant. Many different varieties have been recorded but these are seldom encountered in cultivation.

□ Choice ferns and mosses □

It is difficult to know where to draw the line between a dependable fern and a choice one, for many have both qualities. Those that I am about to introduce are some of the more unusual, sophisticated and sometimes difficult of culture, although the majority will happily live in the rough and tumble of the average garden. All are worth considering, even if you only have a small garden, and some are so striking that they cannot be ignored. Mosses are included here as they require specialist attention, often similar treatment to that advocated for some of the more interesting fern selections which I am about to make.

The most interesting fern that any gardener can grow is the walking fern, *Camptosorus rhizophyllus*, a charming little fellow which produces successions of shiny heart-shaped fronds in a manner which suggests steps. The individual fronds are about 15 cm (6 in) long and borne on reddish frond stalks. Not one of the easiest to grow, for it requires a free-draining medium and dislikes winter damp, but it should be in the collection of any fern enthusiast.

So too should the hardy climbing fern, *Lygodium palmatum*. An eastern North American species, it is the only one of a predominantly tropical family of ferns which can be planted outside with any safety. But even this appreciates a light covering of straw or bracken during the winter months until well established. The quaint heart-shaped leaflets are liberally produced along thin wiry stems, which during a good season will grow to a length of some 1.2 m (4 ft) and quickly festoon any bush within reach. It is easily increased from spores, which are produced in abundance on curious little catkin-like fructifications during early autumn.

■ *Maidenhair ferns*

The adiantums or maidenhair ferns are some of the loveliest. Despite the fact that the majority of the family are not frost hardy, there are at least three beautiful species, which can be grown successfully outdoors. The finest of these is unquestionably the rose-fronded maidenhair, *Adiantum japonicum*, an exquisite little fern capable of bestowing its oriental charm on the dullest and darkest of corners. The dainty, almost pendant, fronds emerge during early spring and are a pleasant shade of rose-pink. As the summer progresses, however, these change through bronze to soft green.

The Kashmir maidenhair, *A. venustum*, is even smaller and more refined with very leafy fronds which change colour with age from soft green with a metallic sheen to golden-yellow, and finally reddish-brown after the first severe frost. The dead fronds remain in character throughout the winter, their dried-up leaflets clinging to the old stalks in much the same manner as beech foliage clings to a beech hedge.

The hardy maidenhair, *A. pedatum*, is a trifle coarser, but nevertheless a splendid plant for a cool damp corner. A native of North America, it has fronds some 60 cm (2 ft) high with long glistening black wiry stalks which support legions of delicate pale green, kidney-shaped leaflets. A dwarf variety called var. *aleuticum*, is equally attractive, but allegedly tougher.

■ *Oak fern*

Both the oak fern and limestone polypody are very hardy and have similar qualities to the maidenhair ferns – delicate, but weather-proof fronds. The oak fern is *Gymnocarpium dryopteris*, a charming little plant with soft yellowish-

Above: *A bold stand of white astilbes throngs the pool edge. Such solid plantings only rest easy in larger landscapes.*
Opposite: *Handsome rhubarb-like leaves of* Gunnera *at the poolside. A giant South American plant that flourishes in wet soil.*

green fronds some 23 cm (9 in) high that arise from a creeping underground stem which delights in wandering through a stony soil in a shaded part of the garden. The limestone polypody, *G. robertianum*, can be equally well satisfied, colonizing favourable areas quickly with its creeping black rhizome and forming a verdant carpet of similar stature and appearance to that of the oak fern.

■ *Thelypteris*

The gymnocarpiums used to belong to a group of ferns called the thelypteris, so there are many characteristics in both genera that are similar, especially with the beech fern, *Thelypteris phegopteris*. This is a quaint little plant for carpeting beneath trees or clothing a shady pocket on the rock garden. The fronds arise singly from a creeping mat of rhizomes and consist of numerous tiny triangular leaflets supported on wiry stems. It is a fern which seems to do much better in an acid soil in a position where its rootstock can creep undisturbed and with little competition from other plants. The marsh buckler fern, *T. palustris*, is a little more particular, demanding a wet soil that is constantly so. Ideal for the bog garden, it is nevertheless an extremely elegant fern with finely cut fronds, which are produced singly at irregular intervals from a creeping mat of black wiry roots. Both barren and fertile fronds are usually in evidence, the latter often persisting well into the winter.

Although one of the easiest to grow, the hay scented fern, *Dennstaedtia punctilobula*, is still not as widely appreciated as it should be. It produces graceful arching fronds in abundance from a thick carpet of twining wiry rhizomes. The fronds are covered with minute glands which emit a delightful fragrance of newly-mown hay. Dennstaedtia is an excellent ground-cover plant which will tolerate any reasonably damp soil in partial shade. Certainly a fern which no self–respecting fern fancier should be without.

■ *Goldie fern*

The same could be said for the goldie fern, *Dryopteris goldiana* and marginal shield fern, *D. marginalis*. Both are easily grown North American natives which grow well in our cool damp climate. Attaining a height of 1.2 m (4 ft) or more, the goldie fern is of imposing stature with enormous broadly lance-shaped grey-green fronds on long scaly stalks. The marginal shield fern is a trifle more modest, its short lance-shaped fronds looking like a refined version of the male fern and growing from a stout tufted rootstock. The variety *elegans* is almost identical, but with greatly enlarged leaflets.

The hay-scented buckler fern, *D. aemula*, is equally charming. An unassuming plant with fronds that are smothered beneath with distinctive stalkless glands, it emits a fragrance of newly mown hay during warm humid weather, and in the autumn as the fronds start to whither. The rigid buckler fern, *D. villarsii*, looks superficially similar, but only enjoys conditions that can be provided in a rock garden.

■ *Chain fern*

The Virginian chain fern, *Woodwardia virginica*, scrambles about in any direction providing that the soil is wet. Of similar growth to *Onoclea sensibilis* it has broad, olive-green fronds of a soft felty texture which are produced from a stout creeping rootstock. Difficulty may be experienced initially in establishing this species, for it often takes a whole season before starting active growth, and during this waiting period the unwary gardener can do untold damage by poking and prying in the area of the dormant root. But once this dormancy is broken there is no containing the plant, the thick black knotted rootstocks spreading rapidly in all directions in much the same manner as those of the common bracken.

■ *Holly fern*
Such exuberance is rarely shown by the holly fern, *Polystichum lonchitis*, an evergreen with spear-shaped divided fronds with sharply toothed leaflets that have given rise to its common name. A native of stony mountainous haunts, this little fern appreciates a good gritty loam in a position that is not too exposed to drying winds or the effects of prolonged sunshine. This is different from the requirements of the other polystichum, *P. achrostichoides*, which lays claim to the common name holly fern, for it requires a moist organic-rich soil in a cool shady place. A native of North America, it too is reliably evergreen, the fronds being garnered in great quantities for Christmas decorations. The dark-green fronds are lance-shaped, coarse-growing and of a glossy and leathery texture. In spring the emerging fronds are covered in glistening white felty scales, but these disappear completely as the summer wears on. A similar and occasionally encountered species, the American sword fern, *P. munitum*, was formerly grown quite extensively for similar purposes and this has long, narrow and quite prickly evergreen fronds.

□ Mosses □

Ferns have been long cultivated in European countries, but mosses are a different proposition. Although a number have been regularly grown, the expertise in cultivating these plants is mostly in Japan where moss gardens are a particular speciality. The climate also has a considerable bearing upon their success, gardeners in cool damp areas finding it easier to maintain neat tight growth, than in warm, dry parts of the country, although the club mosses will grow in most places if given a little shade.

■ *Club mosses*
The common club moss, *Lycopodium clavatum*, is the most frequently encountered, a delicate fellow with dark green ascending branches with narrow, incurved leaflets up to 30 cm (1 ft) or so long. The fir club moss, *L. selago* is somewhat shorter, rarely more than 10 cm (4 in) high. This has forked branches of neat dark green leaflets which form an even carpet. *Lycopodium alpinum* is a similar proposition, being scarcely 10 cm (4 in) high and making neat, tight growth. None of the club mosses have high nutrient requirements and therefore do not respond well to artificial fertilizer. A very peaty mixture is ideal, most species also colonizing well established features made from compressed peat blocks.

■ *Selaginellas*
Selaginellas are related to lycopodiums, and although the majority are commonly grown as house plants, there are a couple of species that are perfectly hardy. Looking rather more like ferns than mosses, and sporting handsome spreading, dark green branching foliage they are more easily cultivated than most of their primitive relatives. An ordinary peaty soil suits

them well, particularly where generous shade can be provided, although I have seen the densely matted *Selaginella helvetica* prospering in a sheltered, damp pocket on the rock garden. For a neat tight carpeting species choose *S. spinosa*, a first class plant for a really damp spot with small, tightly clustered foliage that makes a dense evergreen carpet. Unlike most of their relatives, selaginellas do not resent disturbance, being quite amenable to division and transplanting when necessary.

■ *Cultivation*

Native mosses will naturally invade damp shady areas and the more attractive of these can be nurtured. Not that much needs to be done to encourage their development, for providing the conditions are right they will do the rest. Indeed, they do not respond to regular forms of cultivation, disliking disturbance or the distribution of fertilizers. They hate fallen leaves too, so it is essential during the autumn to remove these before they cause the moss to elongate or turn yellow. Birds love moss, or at least the tiny insects which it harbours, and will scratch amongst it and destroy the soft cushions. Repairs are not easy to effect. All that can be done is to fill the holes in it with ordinary garden soil and await the moss closing in. Transplanting moss for such patching jobs is not a success.

The North American wake robin, Trillium grandiflorum, *one of the most rewarding plants for a shady corner in the peat garden.*

PLANT PROBLEMS

All aspects of gardening have their problems, but fewer afflict the waterside, peat garden or fernery than almost any others. When problems do appear it is as well to be prepared to tackle them straight away.

□ Waterlily aphids □

Waterlily aphids are the most frequent assailants of succulent waterside plants, breeding at a prodigious rate, especially during warm humid weather. They attack all manner of waterside plants, but especially arrowheads and water plantains which seem to attract them like magnets. In the decorative garden, they are the waterside's equivalent of the black bean aphis of the vegetable plot, look rather similar and attack flowers and foliage with impunity. Eggs from the late summer brood of adults are laid on the branches of plum and cherry trees during early autumn and it is here that they overwinter. The eggs hatch during the following spring and winged adult females migrate to waterside plants. Here they reproduce asexually, giving birth to live wingless females which continue to reproduce every day or two until early autumn when a generation of winged males and females is produced that unite sexually and then fly to the plum or cherry trees to deposit their eggs. Summer spraying with insecticides is difficult as the worst infested plants are always at the water's edge. Plants further up the bank are less likely to be attacked. This close proximity to the water means that chemicals can rarely be used without polluting the water. The only remedy then is to spray infested plants with a strong jet of clear water and knock them into the pool where fish will devour them away. The most reliable method of control is to spray dormant plum and cherry trees in the vicinity with DNOC tar oil wash. This is a very effective ovicide that will kill the overwintering eggs and break the life cycle.

□ Caddis flies □

Caddis flies often make themselves a nuisance too, particularly on true aquatic plants and those right at the waterside. There are over one hundred and eighty different species of these curious insects in Britain alone, all of which feed to some extent upon the foliage of aquatic plants. Many are completely aquatic as larvae, swimming around with little shelters of sticks, sand and pieces of plant surrounding them. Adult flies visit the water in the cool of the evening, depositing large quantities of eggs at a time in a quantity of jelly which swells up immediately it touches the water. It is often attached to waterside plants which serve as an anchor as it trails in the water. After ten days or so, the larvae hatch out and immediately start to construct their protective cases from pond and stream debris, including plants. They have voracious appetites, feeding on the leaves, stems and roots of any plants growing in the water. They eventually pupate in the base of waterside plants, emerging as dull moth-like insects with brownish and greyish wings. There is no control for these pests, but in a water body well stocked with fish they are unlikely to get out of control.

□ Moths □

Another pest that attacks waterside plants is the brown china mark moth, a character with hungry caterpillars which shred the foliage from succulent aquatic and waterside plants. Fortunately it is only able to survive on those plants with foliage that is directly in contact with the water, but amongst the water plantains, arrowheads and star fruit it can be very destructive, chewing and distorting foliage which eventually crumbles. The eggs of the brown china mark moth are laid during late summer on the floating foliage of plants. Within a couple of weeks the caterpillars have hatched out and burrowed into the succulent foliage, later making protective cases out of the leaves. They hibernate throughout the winter, but reappear the following spring to continue feeding before eventually spinning a cocoon and pupating. There is no reliable cure, but whenever leaf debris is seen on the surface of the water their activities should be suspected and the free floating pieces netted out. The beautiful china mark moth is a similar proposition, but infests the stems of plants growing at the water's edge. At present there is no control, except for gathering the silky cocoons attached to the plants.

□ Waterlily beetles □

Waterlily beetles do not attack waterside plants, but are very destructive in the pool to waterlilies and other deep water aquatics with succulent floating foliage. However, it is amongst plants at the water's edge that the adults overwinter, so good autumn hygiene is vital if this pest is not to make itself a nuisance in the pool. When the first frosts have killed off the waterside foliage, cut it back quite severely and clear up all the debris around. Most bog garden and streamside marginal subjects can be cut almost to the ground. Be careful of hollow stemmed rushes and reeds as these will rot off if cut beneath water level, but do not neglect to tidy them up, for of all the waterside plants it is these that are likely to be the overwintering host.

□ Aphids □

There are also one or two pests that cause trouble in the peat garden. As with the waterside, aphids are the greatest problem, but at least here you have a chance to do something about them with insecticides. The best kind to use is a systemic insecticide. Usually based upon a chemical called dimethoate, this is absorbed by the plant's sap stream and translocated throughout. Aphids are sucking insects which pierce tissue and feed on sap. If plants are regularly sprayed with a systemic insecticide, then the sap is permanently lethal. For

lasting protection it is usually necessary to spray every three weeks or so. If you are unhappy about using such pesticides, then try pyrethrum. This is a natural plant derivative which kills by contact. It is not as long lasting and does not serve as a protection, but it is equally as lethal to the pest if it comes into contact with it.

□ Vine weevil □

In recent years in many parts of the country vine weevil has started to make itself a nuisance outside, and the place where these infestations have started has usually been the peat garden. Vine weevils are especially drawn to a peaty medium. Commonly a serious pest of greenhouse plants, vine weevil is no less a problem outside, except that on heavy soils it has not yet adapted to outdoor living. It is not until a plant wilts or is on the point of collapse that you know that anything is wrong. The white grubs of this inconspicuous brown weevil live in the soil and eat the roots of plants until virtually nothing remains. Often they are introduced in the pot balls of newly purchased plants from where they spread out to their neighbours. Dousing plants that are vulnerable with a systemic insecticide helps, for when grubs start eating the plant they then imbibe the poison. Otherwise all that you can do is to work a little HCH dust into the soil. This also helps to control leatherjackets and wireworm.

□ Slugs and snails □

Slugs and snails are always prevalent where conditions are permanently damp, so they will be encountered both at the waterside and in the peat garden. However, it is in the peat garden that they are their most destructive, for the environment here is perfect for their life style. There are many different kinds in various sizes and colours, a few of which feed exclusively upon decaying plant debris. Most are a nuisance though, feeding on living plants and delighting in chewing off emerging shoots. They are not too difficult to control, but a constant war must be waged against them. Modern slug pellets, especially those containing methiocarb are particularly effective, also shaking up the local leatherjacket, millipede and wood louse populations too. The more traditional slug baits, both in liquid and pellet form rely upon metaldehyde. While they are effective, they are not as quick and clean as products with methiocarb as the active ingredient. Scatter the pellets amongst the succulent emerging shoots of vulnerable plants during early spring. If you are concerned about either pets or birds finding them, cover small clusters of pellets, placed close by the plants, with pieces of slate or tile raised slightly on stones so that the slugs and snails can gain access, but birds and pets cannot. It is also possible to trap slugs and snails in an upturned grapefruit half with its contents removed, or by placing a small container, sunk up to its rim, adjacent to the plants and then filling it with beer. Slugs and snails apparently love beer and on investigation slip into it and drown.

Ostrich ferns lend colour and interest to this shady poolside. Even gloomy corners can be enlivened with hardy ferns.

INCREASING YOUR PLANTS

It is not my intention here to give extended instructions about the propagation of waterside and peat-loving plants nor hardy ferns and mosses. There are many books that expand upon the methods that are pertinent to individual plants and plant groups. The following guidance is a brief overview for the gardener who wishes to expand his plantings or provide a few plants for a friend. In the case of divisions, then these are often the result of routine maintenance anyway.

▫ Seed raising ▫

This has its limitations, for many of the plants that I have been describing are cultivars and will not, in any event, come true from seed. Most cultivars must be propagated vegetatively if all their desirable characteristics are to be retained in the next generation. However, seed of species such as *Iris sibirica*, *Primula pulverulenta*, together with *P. florindae* and *Myosotis scorpioides* usually produces uniform plants and is the best method of increasing these plants in quantity.

Although it is possible to raise such plants when sown directly in the open ground outside, better results are obtained from raising them in seed trays or pans with the protection of a cold frame. Most seed is best sown as soon as it ripens, which is fine if you can collect your own fresh, but not a lot of good if you have to depend upon the seedsman. In the former case the seed will be sown during mid to late summer, while packeted seed will of necessity have to be sown during early spring. Whenever you put it in it must go into good compost. It is well worth while purchasing compost rather than depending upon your own garden soil. Not only is your own soil likely to be of poorer structure, but it will also contain pests and pathogens.

While the majority of the plants under consideration prefer a moist, warm, equitable climate in which to germinate, a number benefit from chilling in order to break their dormancy, especially those that are purchased from the commercial seed grower and have been lying around in a packet for some months. What happens in the wild is that if conditions are not suitable for germination when a seed falls to the ground, it is rendered dormant by an inhibitor within. This is not broken until the seed has experienced a winter, the action of frost breaking it from its dormancy in preparation for the coming spring. This effect can be recreated at any time of the year if the seed is sown in the usual way in a pan of seed compost and placed in the freezer for a couple of weeks. Once removed to light and warmth after this treatment they will germinate freely.

The seedlings should be pricked out as soon as large enough to handle, individual seedlings being separated out and planted individually. Ideally seedlings should have their seed leaves expanded before transplanting and the first rough leaf showing. Take care with handling young seedlings as they are very brittle and easily damaged. Never hold them by the stem or root, or damping-off disease is likely to take a hold. Once well established in trays, the plants can be lifted and potted separately prior to planting out. Use a potting compost rather than a seed compost at this stage as the plants will probably remain in the pots for several months before getting out into the open ground and will require nutrients.

□ Root cuttings □

Many waterside plants can be increased from root cuttings. The lovely drumstick primula, *Primula denticulata*, is a fine example. This method of propagation is ideal from many points of view, not least of all the speed with which new plants are produced. In most cases it is the only way of increasing a colour selected from seed raised plants. In seed raised *P. denticulata*, for example, there are always a few excellent strong colours. If seed is saved from them, they will not necessarily come anywhere near true, but from root cuttings they are replicated. Cuttings are taken at any time during the dormant period, the adult plant being lifted and suitable pieces of root removed, before the parent is returned to the garden. The best roots to use are those that are no thicker than a pencil, but not so thin that they are likely to dry out before sprouting. The pieces of root are cut into short lengths and placed horizontally in trays of a compost consisting of equal parts by volume of peat and sharp sand, and then lightly covered, watered and placed in a frame. They should sprout by spring when they can be lifted and potted as individual plants.

□ Division □

Most of the more vigorous waterside plants can be increased by division, and normally this is best undertaken during early spring. Irises are an exception: they should be divided and replanted immediately after flowering. The frequency of division varies from one plant to another. It should be done when plants begin to crowd one another, or where established clumps start to die out in the centre. Of course, from a propagation point of view division can be undertaken when a plant is divisible. Carefully lift the plant to be divided with a fork and remove as much surplus soil as possible. To separate large clumps insert two forks back to back and prise apart. For most plants though, the desirable young, vigorous outer pieces of the clump are readily separated by hand. Never use old woody material as this rarely breaks into growth satisfactorily.

□ Cuttings □

A number of streamside plants are most readily increased from short spring stem cuttings, amongst these the lovely aconitums or monkshoods and the myriad mimulus. Cuttings are most successful if taken from the parent plant while short and stocky. Ensure that each cutting has solid tissue, because with subjects like the aconitums they can be hollow and difficult to root. Use a hormone rooting powder to dress the cut end of the shoot for this not only initiates rapid rooting, but helps to prevent rotting as the rooting powder almost always has a fungicide added. To aid rooting it is also useful to make the cut at a leaf joint, for it is here that the cells that are responsible for initiating roots are most numerous. By taking the cutting at a leaf joint a greater number of these cells is exposed. If close conditions are maintained, together with a stable equable temperature, then the cuttings should root quite speedily. It is important following rooting that they are carefully weaned so that they become independent plants without a check in growth.

□ Spore raising □

While many ferns can be increased satisfactorily from division, and it is indeed desirable that the fancy forms are increased in this way, spore raising is still the only satisfactory way of speedily increasing some of the more desirable species, especially those that do not divide freely. Before you embark upon this enterprise it is essential that you appreciate that fern spores are not the flowering plant's exact equivalent of seeds and therefore different growing conditions are required. With most ferns the spores are borne on the undersides of the fronds, although in a few cases they are arranged in dense colonies on separate female fronds, rather like fruiting bodies, which I suppose in some ways they are. When ripe, the spores are cast on the wind and it is at this time that they should be collected and sown. The best way of gathering spores is to place a clean, empty paper bag over a fertile frond, bending it down and snapping it off in the bag. Given a shake the spores will fall like fine pepper dust to the bottom of the bag.

There are many ways of raising spores, but for the gardener without special facilities the following method is easy to achieve success with for most of the hardy ferns which I have described. Sterilized pans, preferably clay, are filled with a compost consisting of three parts by volume peat, one part loam and a pinch of crushed charcoal, this latter being used to keep the mixture sweet. The whole surface of a pan filled with this compost is liberally covered with a layer of crushed brick dust. The pan is stood in a saucer of water, watered thoroughly and then the spores are sown on to the surface in the same way that you might sow fine flower seed such as that of petunias. A small square of glass is then placed over the top of the pan.

In a week or two the surface of the brick dust will become invaded by a green growth rather like a moss. These are the microscopic prothalli of the fern and are either male or female. In close damp conditions these unite to form embryos which then germinate and produce young fern plants. As soon as these baby ferns are recognizable the glass should be removed so that air can circulate. When the plantlets are large enough to handle they can be potted up like seedling herbaceous plants.

A cool moist corner is ideal for hardy ferns. The introduction of hostas with their bold leaves provides solid contrast.

MOISTURE-LOVING PLANTS

1 ■ Mosses and allies

NAME	FLOWER/FOLIAGE	HEIGHT	SPREAD
Lycopodium	green/evergreen	15–30 cm (6 in–1 ft)	15–30 cm (6 in–1 ft)
Selaginella	green/evergreen	15–30 cm (6 in–1 ft)	15–30 cm (6 in–1 ft)

2 ■ Peat garden plants

NAME	FLOWER/FOLIAGE	SEASON	HEIGHT	SPREAD
Arum/Arisaema	green/purple/white brown	summer	30–60 cm (1–2 ft)	30–45 cm (1–1½ ft)
Calluna	white/red/pink	summer	30–60 cm (1–2 ft)	30–45 cm (1–1½ ft)
Cassiope	white	summer	30–60 cm (1–2 ft)	30–45 cm (1–1½ ft)
Cypripedium	yellow/brown/pink/white	summer	30–75 cm (1–2½ ft)	30–45 cm (1–1½ ft)
Dactylorchis	purple	summer	45–75 cm (1½–2½ ft)	30 cm (1 ft)
Erica	white/purple/red	spring/summer/ winter	30–60 cm (1–2 ft)	30–45 cm (1–1½ ft)
Gaultheria	white flowers/ pink fruits	summer/ autumn	15–75 cm (6 in–2½ ft)	30–60 cm (1–2 ft)
Helleborus	white/pink/purple green	winter/spring	30–75 cm (1–2½ ft)	30–45 cm (1–1½ ft)
Lilium	white/pink/orange yellow/red	summer	30 cm–1.5 m (1–5 ft)	30–45 cm (1–1½ ft)
Meconopsis	blue/purple/white red/yellow/orange	summer	30 cm–1.5 m (1–5 ft)	30–45 cm (1–1½ ft)
Phyllodoce	purple	summer	30–60 cm (1–2 ft)	30–45 cm (1–1½ ft)

NAME	FLOWER/FOLIAGE	SEASON	HEIGHT	SPREAD
Podophyllum	white flowers/ red fruits	summer/ autumn	45–75 cm (1½–2½ ft)	30–45 cm (1–1½ ft)
Rhododendron (dwarf)	white/yellow/blue pink/purple	spring	30 cm–1.2 m (1–4 ft)	30–90 cm (1–3 ft)
Rodgersia	white flowers/ green/bronze foliage	summer	60 cm–1.2 m (2–4 ft)	30–75 cm (1–2½ ft)
Sanguinaria	white	spring	15 cm (6 in)	15–30 cm (6 in–1 ft)
Trillium	white/pink/red yellow	spring	15–45 cm (6 in–1½ ft)	15–30 cm (6 in–1 ft)

3 ■ Flowering bog garden plants

NAME	FLOWER/FOLIAGE	SEASON	HEIGHT	SPREAD
Aconitum	blue/yellow/white	summer	90 cm–1.5 m (3–5 ft)	30–60 cm (1–2 ft)
Aruncus	white	summer	60 cm–1.5 m (2–5 ft)	60–90 cm (2–3 ft)
Astilbe	white/pink/red	summer	60 cm–1.2 m (2–4 ft)	30–60 cm (1–2 ft)
Butomus	pink	summer	60–90 cm (2–3 ft)	30 cm (1 ft)
Caltha	yellow/white	spring	15–90 cm (6 in–3 ft)	15–30 cm (6 in–1 ft)
Cardamine	lilac	spring	30–45 cm (1–1½ ft)	15–30 cm (6 in–1 ft)
Eupatorium	purple/white	summer	60 cm–1.2 m (2–4 ft)	30–60 cm (1–2 ft)
Filipendula	white/pink	summer	60 cm–1.8 m (2–6 ft)	45–75 cm (1½–2½ ft)
Iris	blue/purple/white yellow/pink	summer	30 cm–1.5 m (1–5 ft)	30–90 cm (1–3 ft)
Ligularia	orange/yellow	summer	90 cm–1.5 m (3–5 ft)	60–75 cm (2–2½ ft)
Lysichiton	white/yellow green foliage	spring	60 cm–1.2 m (2–4 ft)	30–60 cm (1–2 ft)
Lysimachia	white/yellow	summer	30–60 cm (1–2 ft)	30–45 cm (1–1½ ft)
Lythrum	red/pink	summer	60–90 cm (2–3 ft)	30–45 cm (1–1½ ft)
Menyanthes	white	spring	15–30 cm (6 in–1 ft)	30–45 cm (1–1½ ft)
Mimulus	red/yellow/pink	summer	15–45 cm (6 in–1½ ft)	15–30 cm (6 in–1 ft)
Peltiphyllum	pink flowers bronze-green foliage	spring	90 cm–1.2 m (3–4 ft)	30–45 cm (1–1½ ft)

NAME	FLOWER/FOLIAGE	SEASON	HEIGHT	SPREAD
Pontederia	blue	summer	60 cm–1.2 m (2–4 ft)	30–60 cm (1–2 ft)
Primula	red/pink/orange/ white/purple/lilac	summer	15–75 cm (6 in–2½ ft)	15–30 cm (6 in–1 ft)
Symplocarpus	purple flowers bright green foliage	spring	60 cm–1.2 m (2–4 ft)	30–60 cm (1–2 ft)
Trollius	orange/yellow	spring	15–60 cm (6 in–2 ft)	15–30 cm (6 in–1 ft)

4 ■ Moisture-loving foliage plants

NAME	FOLIAGE	SEASON	HEIGHT	SPREAD
Acorus	green/green and cream variegated	summer	60 cm–1.2 m (2–4 ft)	30–60 cm (1–2 ft)
Alisma	green	summer	60–90 cm (2–3 ft)	30–45 cm (1–1½ ft)
Gunnera	green	summer	1.5–2.4 m (5–8 ft)	1.5–2.4 m (5–8 ft)
Hosta	green/blue/ variegated	summer	60–75 cm (2–2½ ft)	30–60 cm (1–2 ft)
Houttuynia	green/purple	summer	30–45 cm (1–1½ ft)	30 cm (1 ft)
Peltandra	green	summer	60–90 cm (2–3 ft)	30–60 cm (1–2 ft)
Petasites	green	summer	90 cm–1.5 m (3–5 ft)	90 cm–1.5 m (3–5 ft)
Phormium	green/purple/gold	all year round	45 cm–1.8 m (1½–6 ft)	60–90 cm (2–3 ft)
Rheum	green/purple	spring/summer	90 cm–1.8 m (3–6 ft)	90 cm–1.8 m (3–6 ft)
Rumex	green	summer	60 cm–1.5 m (2–5 ft)	30–90 cm (1–3 ft)
Sagittaria	green	summer	60 cm–1.5 m (2–5 ft)	30–60 cm (1–2 ft)

5 ■ Pool edging plants

NAME	CHARACTERISTICS	SEASON	SPREAD
Ajuga	green/maroon/variegated foliage	summer	30–60 cm (1–2 ft)
Cotula	yellow flowers	summer	30–45 cm (1–1½ ft)

Victorian ferns decorate this moss clothed, rock work while marsh pennywort makes a green mound in the centre.

NAME	CHARACTERISTICS	SEASON		SPREAD
Hypericum	yellow flowers	summer		30–45 cm (1–1½ ft)
Lysimachia	green foliage/yellow flowers	summer		30–60 cm (1–2 ft)
Myosotis	blue flowers	summer		30 cm (1 ft)
Preslia	blue flowers	summer		30–45 cm (1–1½ ft)
Saururus	green foliage/white flowers	summer		30–60 cm (1–2 ft)

6 ■ Grasses and bamboos

NAME	FLOWER/FOLIAGE	SEASON	HEIGHT	SPREAD
Arundinaria	green foliage	all year round	30 cm–2.4 m (1–8 ft)	to 90 cm (3 ft)
Arundo	green/cream variegated foliage	all year round	90 cm–2.4 m (3–8 ft)	to 90 cm (3 ft)
Glyceria	green/cream variegated foliage	summer	30–90 cm (1–3 ft)	30–60 cm (1–2 ft)
Miscanthus	green/variegated foliage	summer	60 cm–1.8 m (2–6 ft)	60–75 cm (2–2½ ft)
Pennisetum	silver	summer	90 cm (3 ft)	30–45 cm (1–1½ ft)
Phragmites	green/variegated foliage	summer	90 cm–1.8 m (3–6 ft)	to 90 cm (3 ft)
Phyllostachys	green/gold foliage	all year round	30 cm–1.8 m (1–6 ft)	to 90 cm (3 ft)
Sasa	green foliage	all year round	90 cm–1.8 m (3–6 ft)	to 90 cm (3 ft)
Shibataea	green foliage	all year round	90 cm–1.8 m (3–6 ft)	to 90 cm (3 ft)
Stipa	fawn	summer	45–90 cm (1½–3 ft)	30 cm (1 ft)
Zizania	green foliage	summer	90 cm–3 m (3–10 ft)	30 cm (1 ft)

7 ■ Rushes and reeds

NAME	FLOWER/FOLIAGE	SEASON	HEIGHT	SPREAD
Carex	green/gold foliage	summer	30–90 cm (1–3 ft)	30–45 cm (1–1½ ft)
Cyperus	green foliage	summer	30 cm–1.2 m (1–4 ft)	30–45 cm (1–1½ ft)
Eriophorum	white	summer	30–45 cm (1–1½ ft)	30 cm (1 ft)

NAME	FLOWER/FOLIAGE	SEASON	HEIGHT	SPREAD
Juncus	green foliage	summer	30–60 cm (1–2 ft)	30 cm (1 ft)
Scirpus	green/green/cream variegated foliage	summer	90 cm–1.8 m (3–6 ft)	30–45 cm (1–1½ ft)
Typha	brown	summer	45 cm–1.8 m (1½–6 ft)	to 90 cm (3 ft)

8 ■ Shrubby swamp plants

NAME	CHARACTERISTICS	SEASON	HEIGHT	SPREAD
Cornus	red/yellow stems	winter	90 cm–1.2 m (3–4 ft)	90 cm–1.2 m (3–4 ft)
Salix	orange/violet stems grey foliage	winter	90 cm–1.2 m (3–4 ft)	90 cm–1.2 m (3–4 ft)
Taxodium	green foliage	summer	6–9 m (20–30 ft)	1.8 m (6 ft)
Vaccinium	orange/red foliage	autumn	90 cm–1.5 m (3–5 ft)	90 cm–1.2 m (3–4 ft)

9 ■ Ferns

NAME	FOLIAGE	HEIGHT	SPREAD
Adiantum	green/rose	15–60 cm (6 in–2 ft)	15–60 m (6 in–2 ft)
Asplenium	green/semi-evergreen	15–60 cm (6 in–2 ft)	15–30 cm (6 in–1 ft)
Athyrium	green	30 cm–1.2 m (1–4 ft)	30–60 cm (1–2 ft)
Cystopteris	green	15–45 cm (6 in–1½ ft)	15–30 cm (6 in–1 ft)
Dryopteris	green	30 cm–1.5 m (1–5 ft)	30–75 cm (1–2½ ft)
Matteucia	green	60–90 cm (2–3 ft)	30–45 cm (1–1½ ft)
Onoclea	green	30–60 cm (1–2 ft)	30–60 cm (1–2 ft)
Osmunda	green/purple	60 cm–1.5 m (2–5 ft)	60–90 cm (2–3 ft)
Pellaea	green/purple	15–45 cm (6 in–1½ ft)	15–30 cm (6 in–1 ft)
Polypodium	green/semi-evergreen	15–45 cm (6 in–1½ ft)	15–30 cm (6 in–1 ft)
Polystichum	green/evergreen and semi-evergreen	30–75 cm (1–2½ ft)	30–45 cm (1–1½ ft)
Thelypteris	green	15–75 cm (6 in–2½ ft)	15–30 cm (6 in–1 ft)

INDEX

Acanthus mollis, 67
  spinosus, 67
Aconitum lycoctonum, 33, 121
  napellus, 33, 121
  volubile, 33, 121
  wilsonii, 33, 121
Acorus calamus, 58–60, 122
Adiantum japonicum, 105, 125
  pedatum, 105, 125
  venustum, 105, 125
Ajuga genevensis, 61, 122
  pyramidalis, 61, 122
  reptans, 61, 122
Alchemilla mollis, 67
Alisma parviflora, 60, 122
  plantago-aquatica, 60, 122
Anemone hepatica, 88
  rivularis, 33
  virginiana, 33
Anemopsis californica, 29–31
Anthericum liliago, 36
Apache beads, 29–31
Arisaema candidissima, 91, 120
  triphyllum, 91, 120
Arum crinitum, 92, 120
  dioscoridis, 92, 120
  italicum, 92, 120
    var. *marmoratum*, 92, 120
  maculatum, 92, 120
Aruncus dioicus, 32, 121
  'Kneiffii', 32, 121
  sylvester, 32, 121
Arundinaria anceps, 49, 50, 124
  gigantea, 49, 124
  japonica, 49, 50, 124
  murielae, 49, 124
  nitida, 49, 124
  pumila, 49, 124
  quadrangularis, 49, 124
  simonii, 49, 124
  viridistriata, 49, 124
Arundo donax, 48, 124
Asclepias incarnata, 34
Asplenium ruta-muraria, 104, 125
  trichomanes, 104, 125
  viride, 104, 125
Aster puniceus, 36
Astilbe, 8, 20, 31, 32, 121
  astilboides, 32, 121

chinensis pumila, 32, 121
  crispa, 32, 121
  japonica, 32, 121
  sinensis, 32, 121
  thunbergii, 32, 121
Athyrium filix-femina, 99–100, 125

Bamboos, 49
Beech fern, 108
Blechnum penna-marina, 104
  spicant, 104
Bloodroot, 92
Blueberries, 37
Bog bean, 21–22
Bog garden, construction, 13–17
  creating, 19
  natural, 8
  plants, 20–39
Brooklime, 45, 64
Bugle, 61
Bulrush, 54–55
Buphthalmum salicifolium, 36
  speciosum, 36
Bur reed, 54
Butomus umbellatus, 34, 121

Caddis fly, 112
Calla palustris, 61
Calluna vulgaris, 78–80, 120
Caltha leptosepala, 21, 121
  palustris, 21, 121
  polypetala, 21, 121
Camptosorus rhizophyllus, 105
Cardamine pratensis, 22, 121
Carex morrowii 'Variegata', 53, 124
  pendula, 53, 124
  pseudo-cyperus, 53, 124
  riparia, 53, 124
Cassiope, 84, 120
Convolvulus aureus superbus, 65
  pentapetaloides, 65
  tricolor, 65
Cornish heath, 80–81
Cornus alba 'Sibirica', 36, 125
  stolonifera 'Flaviramea', 36, 125
Cotton grass, 56
Cotula coronopifolia, 64, 122
Cross-leaved heather, 81
Cuckoo flower, 22

Cuttings, 117–8
  root, 117
Cyperus longus, 53, 124
  vegetus, 53, 124
Cypripedium acaule, 93, 120
  calceolus, 93, 120
  japonicum, 93, 120
  pubescens, 93, 120
  reginae, 93, 120
Cystopteris bulbifera, 104, 125
  fragilis, 104, 125

Daboecia cantabrica, 80, 81
Dactylorchis elata, 93, 120
Damasonium alisma, 36
Day lily, 28
Deadnettles, 47
Decodon verticillatus, 60
Dennstaedtia punctilobula, 108
Diphylleia cymosa, 93
Division, 117
Dogwood, 36
Dryopteris aemula, 108
  borreri, 99, 125
  carthusiana, 99, 125
  dilatata, 99, 125
  filix-mas, 97–99, 125
  goldiana, 108
  hexagonoptera, 99, 125
  marginalis, 108
  villarsii, 108

Eomecon chionantha, 93
Epimedium grandiflorum, 47
  pinnatum colchicum, 47
  warleyense, 47
Erica carnea, 80, 120
  cinerea, 80, 120
  darleyensis, 80, 120
  mediterranea, 80, 120
  tetralix, 81, 120
  watsonii, 81, 120
Eriophorum ageratoides, 34, 121
  cannabinum, 34, 121
  fraseri, 34, 121
  perfoliatum, 34, 121
  purpureum, 34, 121

Ferns, 96–108

propagation, 118
Filipendula hexapetala, 28, 121
   kamtschatica, 28, 121
   rubra magnifica, 28, 121
   ulmaria, 28, 121
Foliage plants, 56–60
Fothergilla, 77
Fuchsias, 65

Gaultheria shallon, 83, 120
Geranium endressii, 47
   platypetalum, 47
   psilostemon, 47
Giant reed, 48
Globe flower, 20
Glyceria aquatica, 52, 124
Goat's beard, 32
Grass varieties, 44
Gratiola officinalis, 31
Ground cover plants, 45
Gunnera chilensis, 57, 122
   manicata, 57, 122
Gymnocarpium dryopteris, 105–8
   robertianum, 105–8

Heathers, 78–80
Helleborus abchasicus, 86, 120
   argutifolius, 86, 120
   atrorubens, 85, 120
   foetidus, 85–86, 120
   lividus, 85, 120
   niger, 85–86, 120
   odorus, 86, 120
   orientalis, 86, 120
   × *sternii*, 86, 120
   viridis, 86, 120
Hemerocallis, 28
Hepatica nobilis, 88
Herbicides, 9
Himalayan blue poppy, 84
Hippuris vulgaris, 64
Hosta, 8, 57, 58, 122
   fortunei, 58, 122
   glauca, 58, 122
   lancifolia, 58, 122
   marginata, 57, 122
   plantaginea, 58, 122
   undulata medio-variegata, 57, 122
Houttuynia cordata, 58, 122
Hypericum calycinum, 45, 124
   elodes, 62, 124
   moserianum, 47, 124

Iris, Dutch, 64
Iris aurea, 25, 121
   bulleyana, 24, 121
   chrysographes, 24, 121
   laevigata, 25, 121
   ochroleuca, 25, 121
   pseudacorus, 25, 121
   sanguinea, 24, 121

setosa, 24, 121
sibirica, 24, 121
versicolor, 25, 121

Juncus effusus, 55, 125

Kirengeshoma palmata, 67

Lady fern, 99–100
Lady's mantle, 67
Lady's slipper orchid, 93
Lamium galeobdolon, 47
   maculatum, 47
Ledum groenlandicum, 83
Ligularia clivorum, 33, 121
   hessei, 33, 121
   veitchiana, 33, 121
Limnanthes douglasii, 45
Lilium auratum, 89, 120
   henryi, 89, 120
   martagon, 89, 120
   Mid-Century Hybrids, 89, 120
   regale, 89, 120
   speciosum, 89, 120
   tigrinum, 89, 120
Ling, 78–80
Lobelia cardinalis, 26
   fulgens, 26
   syphilitica, 26
   × *vedrariensis*, 26
Loosestrife, 8, 32
Lycopodium alpinum, 109, 120
   clavatum, 109, 120
   selago, 109, 120
Lygodium palmatum, 105
Lysichiton americanum, 21, 121
   camtschatcense, 21, 121
Lysimachia clethroides, 32, 121
   nummularia, 45, 62, 124
   punctata, 32, 121
Lythrum salicaria, 32, 121
   virgatum, 32, 121

Maidenhair fern, 105
Male fern, 97
Mare's tail, 9, 64
Marsh marigold, 21
Matteucia, 125
May apple, 93
Meadowsweet, 28
Meconopsis betonicifolia, 84, 120
   cambrica, 85, 120
   dhwojii, 85, 120
   from seed, 84–85
   grandis, 85, 120
   horridula, 85, 120
   napaulensis, 85, 120
   regia, 85, 120
Mentha aquatica, 45, 62
Menyanthes trifoliata, 21, 22, 121
Mimulus cardinalis, 25, 121

cupreus, 25, 121
guttatus, 25, 121
lewisii, 25, 121
luteus, 25, 121
ringens, 25, 121
'Whitecroft Scarlet'
Miscanthus sacchariflorus, 52, 124
   sinensis, 52, 124
Monkswood, 33
Mosses, 109–11
Moths, 113
Musk, 25
Myosotis scorpioides, 61, 124

Narthecium ossifragum, 34–36
New Zealand flax, 56

Onoclea, 125
Orchis, 93
Osmunda cinnamomea, 102, 125
   claytoniana, 102, 125
   regalis, 101–2, 125

Parnassia palustris, 36
Peat garden, 68
   building, 72
   construction, 69
   maintenance, 94
   planting, 74–77
   plants, 78–93
   problems, 72
   site, 68
Pellaea, 125
Peltandra alba, 60, 122
   virginica, 60, 122
Peltiphyllum peltatum, 20, 121
Pennisetum alopecuroides, 52, 124
   villosum, 52, 124
Periwinkle, 45
Pernettya, 77
Pests, 112–15
Petasites fragrans, 20, 122
   japonicus, 20, 122
Phormium cookianum, 56, 122
   tenax, 56, 122
Phragmites communis, 48, 124
Phyllitis scolopendrium, 101
Phyllodoce empetriformis, 84, 120
   glandulifera, 84, 120
   × *intermedia*, 84, 120
Phyllostachys aurea, 49, 124
   viridi-glaucescens, 49, 124
Pickerel weed, 34
Pneumatophores, 39
Podophyllum emodi, 93, 121
   peltatum, 93, 121
Polypodium vulgare, 102, 104, 125
Polystichum acrostichoides, 109
   aculeatum, 101, 125
   lonchitis, 109
   munitum, 109

proliferum, 101, 125
setiferum, 101, 125
Pontederia cordata, 34, 122
Pool liners, 17
Preslia cervina, 62, 124
Primula beesiana, 26, 122
bhutanica, 94, 122
bulleyana, 26, 122
chungensis, 26, 122
denticulata, 22, 122
florindae, 26, 122
helodoxa, 28, 122
japonica, 26, 122
microdonta alpicola, 26, 122
pulverulenta, 26, 122
rosea, 22, 122
sieboldii, 94, 122
sikkimensis, 26, 94, 122
viali, 28, 94, 122
Propagation, 116–8
Prothalli, 118

Ranunculus flammula, 34
lingua, 34
Reedmace, 52–53
Reeds, 8
Rheum 'Bowles' Crimson', 20, 57, 122
nobile, 57, 122
palmatum, 20, 57, 122
tanguticum, 20, 57, 122
Rhododendron, dwarf, 77, 83, 121
impeditum, 83, 121
Rodgersia aesculifolia, 92–93, 121
tabularis, 92, 121
Roscoea cautleoides, 88
humeana, 88
Rose of Sharon, 45
Royal fern, 102
Rumex hydrolapathum, 60, 122
Rushes, 8, 55–56

Sagittaria japonica, 58, 122
latifolia, 58, 122
sagittifolium, 58, 122

Salix alba 'Chermesina', 37, 125
babylonica, 37, 125
× *chrysocoma*, 37, 125
daphnoides, 37, 125
lanata, 37, 125
repens, 37, 125
Sanguinaria canadensis, 92, 121
Sanvitalia procumbens, 45
Sasa palmata, 50, 124
tessellata, 50, 124
Saururus cernuus, 62, 124
loureiri, 62, 124
Scirpus lacustris, 54–55, 125
tabernaemontanum, 54–55, 125
Sedges, 8, 53
Seed raising, 116
Selaginella helvetica, 109–11, 120
spinosa, 109–11, 120
Shibataea kumasasa, 49, 124
Shrubs, 36–37
Skunk cabbage, 21
Slugs and snails, 115
Sparganium ramosum, 54
Spearwort, 33–34
Spleenwort, 104
Spore raising, 118
Starfruit, 36
Stipa calamagrostis, 52, 124
pennata, 52, 124
Streamside, 40
diverting flow, 40
erosion, 41
grass, 42
planting, 42
plants, 48
problems, 44–45
Swamp cypress, 39
Sweet flag, 58
Sweet galingale, 53
Symplocarpus foetidus, 21, 122

Taxodium distichum, 39, 125
Thalictrum dipterocarpum, 67
glaucum, 67

speciosissimum, 67
Thelypteris palustris, 108, 125
phegopteris, 108, 125
Thymus lanuginosus, 47
serpyllum, 47
Trenching, 11–13
Trillium erectum, 92, 121
grandiflorum, 92, 121
sessile, 92, 121
stylosum, 92, 121
undulatum, 92, 121
Trollius asiaticus, 20, 122
europaeus, 20, 122
pumilus, 20, 122
yunnanensis, 20, 122
Typha angustifolia, 52–53, 125
latifolia, 53, 125
laxmannii, 53, 125
minima, 53, 125

Vaccinium angustifolium, 37, 125
arboreum, 37, 125
corymbosum, 37, 125
Veronica beccabunga, 45, 64
Vinca major, 45
minor, 45
Vine weevil, 115
Viola cornuta, 47
labradorica, 47
odorata, 47
Water mint, 45, 62
Water plantain, 60
Waterlily aphids, 112
Waterlily beetle, 113
Weed control, 8, 9
Weedkillers, 9
Willow, 36–37
Winter heliotrope, 20
Wood lily, 92
Woodwardia virginica, 108

Zebra rush, 54–55
Zizania aquatica, 54, 124
latifolia, 54, 124

□ Acknowledgements □

The publishers are grateful to the following for granting permission to reproduce the following photographs: Harry Smith Horticultural Photographic Collection (p. 110) and Mrs E. Pyrah (photograph of author on back flap of cover). All the remaining photographs were taken by Bob Challinor.

The photographs on pp. 119 and 123 were taken by kind permission of the Director, Hever Castle, Edenbridge, Kent.

The drawings depicted in Figs. 1 – 5 were drawn by Nils Solberg. The drawing depicted on the chapter openers (*Lysimachia nummularia*) was drawn by Rosemary Wise.